... by Ebury Press, an imprint of Ebury Publishing

...se Group Company

...© Miss Hope 2011
...© Ebury Press 2011

...s asserted her right to be identified as the author of this Work
...e with the Copyright, Designs and Patents Act 1988

...erved. No part of this publication may be reproduced, stored
...I system, or transmitted in any form or by any means, electronic,
..., photocopying, recording or otherwise, without the prior
... of the copyright owner

...om House Group Limited Reg. No. 954009

...es for companies within the Random House Group can be found at
...andomhouse.co.uk

...catalogue record for this book is available from the British Library

...andom House Group Limited supports The Forest Stewardship Council
...), the leading international forest certification organisation. All our titles
...are printed on Greenpeace approved FSC certified paper carry the
...logo. Our paper procurement policy can be found at www.rbooks.co.uk/
...ironment

...buy books by your favourite authors and register for offers visit
...ww.rbooks.co.uk

...rinted and bound in China by Toppan Printing Co., (SZ) Ltd

ISBN 9780091940393

Every effort has been made to contact the copyright holders. Please contact
the publishers with any queries. Please note that conversions to imperial
weights and measures are suitable equivalents and not exact.

Design: Smith & Gilmour
Photography: Cristian Barnett and Dan Jones
Styling: Miss Hope
Food styling: Emma Marsden

For Jake, I am so proud of you.
RRLYxxx

10 9 8 7 6 5 4 3

Published in 20

A Random Ho

Text copyrigh
Photography

Miss Hope
in accordan

All rights r
in a retrie
mechanic
permissio

The Ran

Addres
www.r

A CIP

The
(FSC
that
FSC
en

T
v

CONTENTS

HELLO CHUMS!

Hello Chums, this is the fragrant Miss Hope speaking to you from the sticky topped table, sugar-sprinkled Hope and Greenwood kitchen. Beyond my window the summer is rolling by, clouds travel the periwinkle sky, ripe cows are mumbling a sugar-brown hymn, cobble clipping hooves clatter in the dairy. Yes, South London is truly idyllic.

I am the Hope bit of Hope and Greenwood – you may call me Hopey, but only if I like you . . . The other half is the moustache-twirling Mr Greenwood. Stocky as a bulldog, brave as a badger, whiskered as a weasel. That is Mr G. Colourful of both shirt and language, broad of both chest and mind. Lover of pies, quaffer of Rioja and avid reader of the Bravissimo catalogue. Sometimes we are married, though this largely depends on who is asking.

'Hope and Greenwood is the finest confectioner in Britain,' says my mum – and she is quite right. If you are a Londoner you may already frequent the Hope and Greenwood sweet shops; their walls lined with 200 glass jars of fabulous confectionery, old and new. Ginger Beer Humbugs, Sugar Plums and Fizz! Bang! Wallops! The H & G counter is fecund with Bucks Fizz Truffles, oozing Honey Caramels, Raspberry and Champagne Truffles, Rum, Whisky and Amaretto chocolates. The discerning of you will already be mad for our Coffee and Walnut, Lemon Meringue, Treacle Tart, Spotted Dick and Chocolate Fudge Cake chocolate bars, inspired by British cakes and puddings of my childhood.

It seems churlish, therefore, being as passionate about chocolate as we are, not to share some of our secrets with you. Some recipes, I confess, had to be dragged out of me like getting Mr G's granddad out of The Gold Diggers Arms. Be reassured by the winning combinations of Ginger

Creams, Pear and Chestnut, and Fig and Cassis Truffles. Be tempted by the titillating flavours of Strawberry and Cream Lollipops, and Chilli and Lime Kisses.

In addition to my delicious truffle recipes you may wish to take a peek into my baking world. When I was still in white socks and braces my mother served 'Ladies' Afternoon Tea' when my father was out 'am' dramming, and only ladies (my sister and I) were invited.

My mother was a Bero cook – that slim, monotone, baking bible for good housewives. Warm scones wrapped in a white napkin with cream and homemade strawberry jam, three-tiered chocolate cakes, prised from their baking tins while still warm and impatiently sandwiched with buttercream and dusted with clouds of icing sugar, chocolate meringues with a hidden silver sixpence wrapped in greaseproof paper, profiteroles filled with cold cream and sploshed with rich chocolate sauce, pretty pink fondant fancies with tiny sugar flowers. There was butter and sugar to be creamed, chocolate to be melted and bowls and spoons to be licked clean. It is little wonder that my love of both home baking and chocolate should manifest itself in a plethora of delicious cakes and fancies (which you will find on pages 106–124).

So, now it is time to get down to business. The day is stretching ahead with so many chocolatey possibilities that it will be evening when we finish, slumped exhausted over a bowl of fondant, a light dusting of cocoa behind your spectacles and chocolate handprints on the dado. Stand up straight and stop slouching, pay attention, look lively, keep your hands on the wheel and your smiles for your mother. Spoons at the ready, tea towels starched, chocolate in the pantry, apron smoothed.

Now, let's begin. *Miss Hope*

WHAT IS CHOCOLATE ANYWAY?

Theobroma cacao is the name of the tree that produces the cacao (or cocoa) bean, whence, eventually, comes chocolate. It grows 20 degrees north and south of the Equator, thrusting out large, red, purple, orange and yellow fruit pods. If you open a pod, inside you will discover the seed of these fruits – the cacao bean. It looks as much like chocolate right now as Mr Greenwood looks like George Clooney. (Oh, Mr G, don't get grumpy, you know I prefer the Ray Winston type.)

Once removed from its pod, the cacao bean is first cleaned then roasted. In the same way that roasting deepens the flavour of coffee beans, so it is for the cacao bean. Once roasted, the bean is pressed between rollers to remove the husk and create the nibs – it is these that are essential to making chocolate.

The next stage is grinding down these nibs. The liquid cocoa mass – which is now pure chocolate in rough form – that comes from this process is then blended with cocoa butter (the pure, edible vegetable fat that comes from the cacao bean) and other ingredients, depending on what type of chocolate is being made.

Dark chocolate is also known as bittersweet, semi-sweet or sweet dark or plain chocolate. It contains at least 35 per cent cocoa solids, but more fashionably it is made from 70 per cent cocoa solids and no or very little milk; the more cocoa solids used in the chocolate, the richer the flavour will be. Dark chocolate is traditionally made from cocoa solids, cocoa butter, a much smaller amount of milk powder than milk chocolate, sugar, and any specific flavourings, such as vanilla.

Milk chocolate should officially contain a minimum of 25 per cent cocoa solids and is made up of these plus cocoa butter and milk (in the form of powdered, liquid or condensed milk), sugar, and any other flavourings.

White chocolate is called chocolate but it isn't really as it doesn't contain any cocoa mass. In fact it is made from cocoa butter, sugar, milk solids and vanilla, and lecithin is added in commercial products (it is an emulsifier which helps to keep all the ingredients together).

Couverture chocolate is available in dark, milk and white, but has a higher cocoa butter content than ordinary chocolate (usually 36–39 per cent). It's used in chocolate-making when you want to encase them in a shell, such as the seashell caramels on page 38, and can be found in supermarkets or online (please see the end of this book for stockists). Because of its higher cocoa butter content it's easier to use, will spread more easily and makes a lovely thin shell.

Once the chocolate type being made has been determined and the relevant ingredients have been added, the next stage is conching. This is the key process that produces cocoa and sugar particles that are smaller than the tongue can detect, during which butter and sugar are mixed together at a controlled temperature to produce a lovely smooth texture and flavour.

The final stage in making chocolate is tempering. Please see page 13 for an explanation of this.

WHAT'S LOVE GOT TO DO WITH IT?

Chocolate contains anandamide, which is calming; theobromine, which gives us a mental boost; phenylethylamine, which stimulates the nervous system and increases heart rate; and tryptophan, which aids the production of the serotonin, which makes you calm. Best of all, chocolate triggers the release of endorphins, which reduce the chocolate lover's sensitivity to pain and results in that warm inner glow.

Taking all that into consideration, it is not surprising that chocolate makes us feel all loved up, as if Colin Firth just knocked at the door waggling a bottle of Babycham and a kebab having just returned from a desert island where he has spent 10 long celibate years.

HOW TO TASTE CHOCOLATE

Like all good things, it takes a little time to learn how to taste chocolate properly. Isn't that fabulous? Tasting chocolate is like tasting wine; there are subtleties of bean and location, of quality and content, married with the overwhelming desire to just eat as much of it as you can in one sitting.

Firstly you need to be nice and relaxed so that all your senses are aware – make sure you are wearing your cashmere lounging pyjamas and your hair is shiny. A cleansed palate is essential, too, so steer clear of coffee or tea before you taste. If you're lucky and are trying more than one type, start with the chocolate with the lowest percentage of cocoa solids first. Dark chocolate is strong and powerful and you don't want the flavours to be clashing like yellow shoes with a green dress when you taste the other bars.

Take a decent-sized piece and look at the colour of it – yes, yes, I know, it is brown, but look closer, it should be free from any white marks (known in the trade as 'bloom').

Now give it a good lingering sniff and see if you can identify any of the complex flavours within.

Next, hold the piece between your hands and break it in half – you should hear a good 'SNAP'. If it does this, the quality is top notch.

Put a piece on your tongue and really try to resist biting and chewing it (I know it is hard, but give it your best shot) – just let the chocolate slowly melt. As the chunk dissolves into saucey goodness in your mouth you'll start to taste all those rich flavours.

A good-quality bar will have a smooth silky texture; a rubbish one will leave a grainy finish. Flavours range from hay, wood, mushrooms, moss, fruity orange and red berries to others such as toast, butter and honey, liquorice and honey, caramel, coffee and nuts. If the taste isn't fresh and it seems stale or metallic, you've got a poor-quality chocolate.

HOW AND WHY TO TEMPER CHOCOLATE

If you heat and cool chocolate without controlling the temperature the crystallisation of cocoa butter will result in crystals of different sizes (bad crystals) forming, and your chocolate will bloom – that is to say it will appear matt and covered with white patches. It will also crumble unpleasantly rather than snap. In order to avoid this you will need to temper your chocolate.

Tempering controls the crystals so that only consistently small crystals are produced, resulting in much better-quality chocolate. I have, wherever possible, avoided the need to temper chocolate completely by rolling my truffles in sugar, cocoa or nuts, but if the recipe requires it and you want your chocolate to be shiny 'snapable', without a white bloom, then temper you must.

When making moulded chocolates that are filled with ganache or a fruity cream filling, you need to use couverture chocolate, such as Callebaut or Valrhona, which has a higher cocoa butter content but which does need to be tempered (please see the end of this book for stockists). This will give the chocolates a lovely appetising shine, a pleasing snap when you bite into it and a smooth, melt-in-the-mouth texture without any graininess. If you use regular chocolate the finished chocolates won't look as polished and the shell may crack or look a bit waxy.

For all my recipes that require the chocolate to be tempered, please use 300g (11oz) of couverture chocolate for one tray of chocolates and about 450g (1lb) of couverture chocolate for two trays. These quantities will ensure the temperature of the chocolate is maintained while you coat the moulds. Don't worry if you don't use all the tempered chocolate, as you can scrape it into a container, seal it, store it at room temperature and use it later. Before reusing the chocolate, temper it again if you are using it for chocolate shells, or melt it in a bain marie if you're using it to make truffles.

TEMPERING FOR RICH PEOPLE
The easiest but priciest way of tempering chocolate is to buy a tempering machine. This heats up the chocolate very, very slowly then cools it down equally slowly, leaving the finished chocolate silky smooth.

THE TRICKY METHOD FOR SMARTY PANTS PEOPLE

This is a bit of a faff as you need a slab of marble, a thermometer and a metal scraper, thick palette knife or spatula.

First you need to melt the chocolate very gently in a heatproof bowl set over a pan of warm water – making sure the chocolate doesn't overheat and the bottom of the bowl doesn't touch the water. Then pour around three-quarters of the melted chocolate onto the marble slab. Work it across the slab until it has reached a temperature of 28°C (82°F) – this is where you need to stick the thermometer into the chocolate all over the slab. Using your scraper/palette knife/spatula, scrape the chocolate back into the bowl with the rest of it. Heat all the chocolate very gently, if necessary, or allow the residual heat to bring it back up to a temperature of 31–32°C (88–90°F) for dark chocolate, 30–31°C (86–88°F) for milk chocolate and 27–28°C (80–82°F) for white chocolate. It's now ready to use. Good luck.

THE MIDDLE GROUND FOR PEOPLE WITH A SOCIAL LIFE

If you're going to be making chocolates a lot, buy a chocolate thermometer. They're not very expensive and they will make it easier to temper chocolate accurately.

Chop your chocolate evenly and put about two-thirds of it in a heatproof bowl. Heat 5cm (2in) water in a pan and pop the bowl on top of the pan, making sure that the bottom of the bowl is not touching the water. Allow the chocolate to melt slowly.

Once it's liquid, turn off the heat, remove the bowl from the pan and wrap a clean tea towel round the base to keep it warm. Add the remaining chopped chocolate, pop the thermometer in and stir the chocolate until it reaches 31–32°C (88–90°F) for dark chocolate, 30–31°C (86–88°F) for milk chocolate and 27–28°C (80–82°F) for white chocolate. This will take a while. Once done, it's ready to use.

THE MICROWAVE METHOD FOR PEOPLE WITH JOBS, CHILDREN, PETS, FRIENDS, OR A TRAIN TO CATCH

Pop the chopped-up chocolate into a microwaveable plastic or glass bowl and melt at 800–1000W, checking it every 15 seconds or so and taking care it doesn't overheat. When the chocolate looks nearly melted but there are still a few bits bobbed on top, take it out of the microwave and stir the chocolate gently until smooth. It should have thickened slightly. It's now ready to use.

THE RULES

Now pay attention as this bit's important. There are rules when it comes to making good chocolate, and rules must be obeyed at all times. Failure to obey the rules will result in hot chocolate on your kaftan, bicarbonate of soda on your burns and a bit of girly weeping into your waffle tea towel. So look lively, read the dos and don'ts and stop blubbering.

★ 1 ★

Please do: Melt chocolate with care. Use as little heat as possible, as this will stop it going white when it sets, which looks horrible. Take particular care with white chocolate, which melts in no time at all and so can burn very easily. It's best to melt couverture chocolate (see page 9) if you're making chocolates that have a shell.

★ 2 ★

Please do: Listen carefully. When I say 'use a deep heavy-bottomed pan' (4 litres or 7 pints big), it is not a joke, a jest or a wicked wheeze. Use it or be damned.

★ 3 ★

Please do: Refrain from eating hot fudge or nougat straight from the pan, you greedy guts. It is really, really hot, it will burn you and you will weep like a Versailles fountain. You need to pour it straight into the tin and wait for it to set. Please do be patient or I will call your mother and tell her you haven't changed at all.

★ 4 ★

Please do: Buy a sugar thermometer; I beg you, as it doesn't cost too much and it is the ideal tool for the job when making fudge and nougat. How many times?

★ 5 ★

Please do: Keep your eye firmly on your cooking. Some of the recipes require you to watch the sugar thermometer closely and stare at the pan with the air of a mad person while they cook. If you don't you'll miss the perfect temperature and you'll be in danger of setting the kitchen alight, then Jean will fly in from next door and catch you cooking in your pants.

★ 6 ★

Please do: Use the right type of paper for baking. You need greaseproof for the cakes and baking parchment for the biscuits and meringues. Don't mix them up or you'll have cakes repelled by the parchment and meringues with a paper bottom as they'll stick to the greaseproof. Don't you know anything? Line your cake tins well with butter and greaseproof and they'll slip off faster than a bride's nightie.

★ 7 ★

Please do: Use a wooden spoon when stirring fudge or nougat. A plastic spatula will melt like the Wicked Witch of the West.

★ 8 ★

Please do: Leave the Brillo pad under the sink. The best way to wash a pan covered in fudge or nougat is to fill it with water and put it back on the heat. The stickiness will just bubble off. Easy peasy.

★ 9 ★

Please do: Enjoy a tot of liqueur if you're making any of the recipes with booze. It'll make the experience so much more pleasurable or, in the case of culinary disaster, forgettable.

★ 10 ★

Please do: Make chocolates and treats for your friends and neighbours – especially Jean and Derek. They will think you actually like them and will stop having bonfires just after you put your washing out.

STORAGE

It would be foolish to suppose that you would store your chocolates at all. If you are like me you may not be able to resist the instant gratification derived from a fresh Limoncello Truffle or a chunk or two of Black Forest Fudge. However, if you are like my skinny friend Sue, who is disciplined and eats neither chocolate nor chips but likes to indulge all those around her, you may wish to store your treats in a sensible way. So here is how.

As a general rule, all chocolates that are being stored in the fridge should be kept in an airtight container to avoid tainting them with the odours of other food near them.

Truffles made with fresh cream should be kept in the fridge and eaten within 3–4 days. If you freeze them they will last two months.

Fudge can be stored in the fridge for up to two weeks, but please remove it from the fridge and allow it to warm to room temperature before you eat it. It will also freeze well for two months.

Nougat should be stored in a cool, dry place for up to two weeks. Putting it in the fridge turns it into a gooey mess and it will ooze unpleasantly, like leprous sores.

Chocolates filled with fresh cream ganache should be kept in the fridge and eaten within 3–4 days. Remove them from the fridge and allow them to warm to room temperature before eating.

Cakes should be stored in an airtight container in a cool place. Don't chill them or the fluffy sponge will turn into a tough-textured flannel. They can be enjoyed within 2 days if filled with fresh cream, or 3 days if filled with buttercream.

Meringues should be stored in an airtight container – unfilled, of course – and will keep for up to 1 month. Once filled with fresh cream they should be devoured immediately.

Profiteroles should be stored in an airtight container – unfilled and un-iced – and will keep for up to 3 days.

Biscuits and Florentines should be stored in an airtight tin and will keep for 2–3 days, otherwise they'll turn soft and soggy.

Chocolate mousse should be stored in the fridge for up to 2 days.

Mr Greenwood If Mr Greenwood got on a bike/wagon and gave up cheese he might last another 30 years. Which would be nice, as I really need him to decorate the spare room.

HOPE AND GREENWOOD
SPLENDID CONFECTIONERY

Truffles and Creams

CHAPTER ONE

PEAR AND CHESTNUT TRUFFLES

★ **Makes 8 chunky truffles**

★ **Take 1 hour to make; plus chilling and overnight setting.**

2 dried pears, finely
   chopped
75ml (3fl oz) pear vodka
4 cooked chestnuts,
   from a packet
100g (3½oz) milk
   chocolate
25g (1oz) unsalted butter
Milk chocolate, for
   tempering
200g (7oz) marzipan
Green food colouring
Icing sugar, for dusting
Dark chocolate, for
   tempering

This autumnal truffle is made with an amazing pear vodka and chestnut ganache wrapped in a scarf of green marzipan, and once enrobed with dark chocolate it looks precisely like a chocolate conker nestling in its prickly case. The autumn wind is whipping through the trees, the sun is low and cool, so take a walk in the park, kick up some leaves, fly a kite, feed the ducks and fight off a mugger.

★ Whap the chopped pears in a pan with the pear vodka and bring to the boil. Drink a bit of vodka. Simmer for 2–3 minutes until the fruit is soft and yielding. Slap the fruity vodka into a mini food processor with the chestnuts and whiz to make a sticky purée.

★ Heat 5cm (2in) water in a pan. Plop a heatproof bowl on top of the pan, making sure the ample bottom of the bowl is not dipping into the water. Place the milk chocolate in the bowl and warm to melt – please don't stir it otherwise it may turn into a great big, thick mess.

★ Now then, when the chocolate has melted beauticiously, drop in the butter with the chestnut and pear purée and stir as gently as a kitten. Spoon the mixture into a bowl and chill until firm. If only this method worked on thighs.

★ Use a teaspoon to scoop out some mixture and shape into small balls the size of marbles. Size is everything. Freeze on a baking sheet covered with baking parchment for 30 minutes to 1 hour.

P.T.O.

★ After that time, temper the dark chocolate (see page 13). Line a board with baking parchment, dip each pear and chestnut ball into the chocolate using a chocolate dipping fork or table fork or somefink, then lift out and plant on the parchment. Whack them in a safe place to set and firm up like Caster Semenya's calves.

★ Knead the marzipan lightly on a board, then drip on a couple of dots of green food colouring (rubber gloves may be worn, if you needed an excuse). Work the food colouring into the marzipan until thoroughly mixed through.

★ Dust the work surface with icing sugar then roll out half the marzipan to make a rough square. Cut into four, then wrap each square around one of the pear and chestnut balls. Cut out a horizontal leaf-shaped oval in each marzipan ball to reveal a little of the chocolate underneath. Trim each with a knife round the base and press to shape around the chocolate. Repeat with the remaining chocolates and marzipan, then leave to set at room temperature for at least 8 hours or overnight.

★ Temper the dark chocolate, as before. Take a chocolate in one hand and a spoon in the other. Spoon the chocolate all over the marzipan, leaving about a 2mm edge around the green marzipan window. Allow the chocolate to go tacky, then take a fork and press and lift it all over the dark chocolate to create a spiky finish. Crack on with covering and spiking up the rest. Once 'punked', allow the chocolate to set.

Trivia

Pyriform means 'shaped like a pear'. As in: 'There is Jean, my nudist neighbour, weeding the back of the beds again. Who ate all the pyriforms?'

CHAMBORD AND RASPBERRY TRUFFLES

Apparently Louis XIV liked a tipple of Chambord, and without doubt would have approved of these truffles fit for a king. They are filled with a dark, rich ganache of raspberries, blackberries, Madagascar vanilla, Moroccan citrus peel, honey and cognac, enrobed with white chocolate and crowned with dried raspberries. If you eat too many you will undoubtedly sprout a big, black, poodle hairdo, a passion for red stockings and a velvet *chapeau* with a *fleur-de-lis* trim.

★ Heat 5cm (2in) water in a pan. Pop a heatproof bowl on top of the pan, making sure the bottom of the bowl is not touching the water. Place the chocolate and cream in the bowl and warm until melted – don't stir it otherwise it may turn into a thick mess like a ditchdrab's hedgerow soup.

★ Meanwhile, push the raspberry jam through a sieve to remove any pips. Stir the sieved jam into the chocolate and cream mixture with the butter and Chambord off the heat until well combined. Chill until as firm as Viv Merduff, my personal trainer.

★ Use a teaspoon to scoop up some truffle mixture and shape it into a ball about the size of a walnut. Line a 39 x 35cm (15¼ x 13¾in) baking sheet with baking parchment, set each truffle on the parchment and repeat until all the mixture is used up.

★ Finely chop the raspberry bits and place on a plate. Roll each truffle in the raspberry bits until they are coated all over and pop the finished chocolates into paper cases. Chill to firm up.

★ **Makes 24 regal truffles**

★ **Take 25 minutes to make; 10 minutes to ponce around like a Sun King.**

150g (5oz) dark chocolate, finely chopped
75ml (3fl oz) double cream
3 tbsp good-quality raspberry jam
25g (1oz) unsalted butter, chopped
2 tbsp Chambord raspberry liqueur
25g (1oz) dried raspberry bits

Sweet Style
I would quite like a hat with a fleur-de-lis trim; 'This hat, c'est moi', etc., etc., and so on and so forth.

FIG AND CASSIS TRUFFLES

My fabulous fig-shaped truffles are made from luscious figs, milk chocolate, a splash of cassis and then rolled in purple sugar.

★ Introduce the figs to the pan, slosh in the cassis and bring to the boil, then simmer for 1 minute. Cool them. Tum te tum. Whiz with abandon into a sumptuous purée – don't worry if there are a few pieces of fig skin, there's nothing wrong with chunky (as my mother used to say).

★ Heat 5cm (2in) water in a pan. Pop a heatproof bowl on top of the pan, making sure the bottom of the bowl is not touching the water. Allow the chocolate and cream to mingle in the bowl until warm and melted – don't stir it otherwise it may turn into a right disaster. Stir in the butter. Stir in the fig mixture then cover and chill for at least 2 hours until as firm as a builder's arm.

★ Sprinkle a couple of tablespoons of caster sugar onto a plate, add a couple of drops of food colouring and rub in with your fingers to colour the sugar.

★ Take a meaningful teaspoonful of the chocolate fig mixture and roll it around between willing palms until all your balls are perky. Shape the mixture, pulling it upwards to make a fig. Repeat with the rest of the mixture to make around 20 fig-shaped truffles.

★ Roll each truffle in the coloured caster sugar to coat. Present them in paper cases if you wish and chill until stiff.

★ **Makes 20 fig-shaped truffles**

★ **Take 25 minutes to make; plus chilling and setting time.**

6 dried figs, chopped
3 tbsp cassis
200g (7oz) milk chocolate
2 tbsp double cream
50g (2oz) unsalted butter
Caster sugar, to dust
A few drops of purple food colouring (or mix together blue and red)

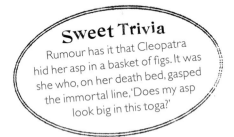

Sweet Trivia
Rumour has it that Cleopatra hid her asp in a basket of figs. It was she who, on her death bed, gasped the immortal line, 'Does my asp look big in this toga?'

CHOCOLATE HAZELNUT PRALINES

★ **Makes around 22 nutty truffles**

★ **Take 25 minutes to make (the same amount of time it takes to get to Willy Weasel's house); plus 1 hour chilling (man!).**

A dribble of vegetable oil
75g (3oz) granulated sugar
75g (3oz) toasted hazelnuts, plus 40g (1½oz) extra to coat
100g (3½oz) milk chocolate, chopped
55ml (2fl oz) double cream
10g (½oz) salted butter, chopped
1 tbsp Frangelica (hazelnut liqueur, fool – all that money I paid for your education.)

Once upon a time, Squirrel Greenwood went hop, skip, jump into the Dark Wood to forage for hazelnuts. Suddenly, from the dark, dank gloom of centuries, the Great Lord of the Green appeared, shaking his fecund boughs of ripe hazelnuts.

'Squirrel Greenwood!' he boomed, 'to pick the nuts from my laden boughs you must first help your mummy with the dishes and hand your homework in on time.'

Squirrel Greenwood straightened his neckerchief and gulped nervously,

'Fo sho, fo shizzle, man, what's poppin ... keep it fresh, yo' feel me and ting?'

And he scampered off to play Ninjas with Willy Weasel.

★ Line a 39 x 35cm (15¼ x 13¾in) baking sheet with baking parchment and brush lovingly with oil. Plonk the sugar and 75g (3oz) hazelnuts in a pan. Heat very gently until the sugar has dissolved, stirring continuously with a wooden spoon. Cook until the sugar turns dark golden of a Gaugin maiden's thigh – as soon as it does, quickly pour onto the oiled parchment and leave to set. When cool, break up into smallish chunks and whiz in a food processor or perhaps a coffee grinder – if you are posh. If you are common, like me, just stick it in a tea towel and whack it with a sturdy rolling pin.

★ Heat 5cm (2in) water in a pan. Pop a heatproof bowl on top of the pan, making sure the bottom of the bowl is not touching the water. Place the chocolate in the bowl with the cream – don't stir it otherwise it may turn into a thick sticky mess and you will write to me and have a moan.

★ When the chocolate has melted, add the butter and Frangelica and the nut mixture and stir together. Chill for at least 1 hour until as firm as a carrot of Monolithic Ceria-stabilized Zirconia.

★ Finely chop the remaining 40g (1½oz) hazelnuts and sprinkle on a plate. Take a teaspoon and scoop up some of the truffle mixture, then roll it between your palms to make a ball the size of a schoolboy's marble. Roll the truffles in the chopped hazelnuts until coated all over, then lay them happily on a sheet of greaseproof paper. Do the same to use up the remaining truffle mixture and nuts until you fall exhausted into the mixing bowl, tongue first.

FUN AND GAMES

You really need three people to play Ninjas – one guard and two ninjas. If you have no friends stick a bath plug on the back of your neck, jump over the sofa and go Matrix.

PASSION FRUIT HEARTS

★ **Makes 24 amorous hearts**

★ **Take about 30 minutes to make; plus chilling and setting time.**

2 passion fruits
25g (1oz) good-quality white chocolate, chopped
1 tbsp double cream
5g (¼oz) unsalted butter
White chocolate, for tempering

2 chocolate mould trays of 12 bite-sized hearts (please see the end of this book for stockists)

Mr Greenwood is often distracted by the fleeting glimpse of a lady's ankle while promenading. My sweet Passion Fruit Hearts are equally tempting and I find myself hiding them in case he gets too giddy. Once, Jean next door hid them for me in her special hiding place and Derek came round and threatened to report Mr Greenwood to the Neighbourhood Watch.

★ Halve the passion fruits and scoop the juice and seeds into a sieve set over a bowl to the tune of 'Once I had a Secret Love'. Use a wooden spoon to stir the seeds round the sieve to push through the juice and any bits of pulp. Throw away the seeds like a discarded lover.
★ Heat 5cm (2in) water in a pan. Plonk a heatproof bowl on top of the pan, making sure the bottom of the bowl is not touching the water. Place the 25g (1oz) of white chocolate with the cream in the bowl and warm tenderly until melted. Remove the bowl from the pan and stir the butter and passion fruit juice into the melted chocolate. Whack it on the windowsill for a bit.
★ Temper the remaining white chocolate (see page 13) and use a clean, grease-free brush or teaspoon to thinly coat and line the moulds with white chocolate. Please do it faster, you are far too slow, if you don't get a move on the chocolate will cool and become as thick as the soft lad that hangs around the chip shop. If you are obsessive–compulsive take a sharp knife or chocolate scraper to tidy up any bits around the chocolate shells. Scrape any white chocolate that

P.T.O.

you haven't used into a bowl and save to use again. Put the moulds in the fridge to set for around 20 minutes.

★ Take the moulds out of the fridge. Spoon a little of the passion-fruit mixture into each heart-shaped mould, leaving a couple of millimetres at the top so there's room to enclose the filling with a layer of white chocolate. Whap back in the fridge to set for about 45 minutes. While you wait go to the spare room window and check if Jean is sunbathing.

★ Temper some more white chocolate or use any that's left over from before (but you might need to add a little more chocolate to it), and, using a teaspoon, cover all of the passion fruit mixture and fill up the moulds. Chill again to set the chocolate.

★ Take the chocolates out of the fridge and upturn the mould trays onto a board – the Passion Fruit Hearts should slip out easily – it is all in the wrist action. Any left behind might need a gentle twist of the mould to release them or coaxing out with the promise of a gin and tonic.

CHOCOLATE GINGER CREAMS

Less Mick Hucknall, more Ginger Rogers, my spicy chocolate-covered Ginger Creams are full of toe-tapping pizzazz. Do feel free, dear chum, to increase or decrease the ginger to your preferred pain threshold. 'Heaven. I'm in heaven, and my mouth burns so that I can hardly speak . . .'

★ Sift the icing sugar into a bowl and add the grated ginger. In a separate bowl, beat the egg white until just frothy, man, and add to the sugar and ginger. Stir everything together – you may wish to sing the little ditty below to the tune of 'Dancing Cheek to Cheek'.
★ Put on a pair of marigolds if you are weedy wet, or simply get stuck in with bare hands and knead the mixture in the bowl until smooth and all the icing sugar has worked its way into the sweet fondant.
★ Pull off walnut-sized pieces. Flatten with the palm of your hand, like an old penny, then place on a 39 x 35cm (15¼ x 13¾in) baking sheet covered with baking parchment and leave to dry out overnight.
★ Chop the extra stem ginger into slivers. Melt the two chocolates in separate heatproof bowls set over pans of boiling water. Using a chocolate dipping fork or table fork, dip half of each ginger cream into either the milk or white chocolate, leaving the other half uncoated. Return the chocolate to the baking parchment and decorate each with a whisper of ginger. Leave to set.

★ **Makes 40**

★ **Take 30 minutes to sling together; plus overnight drying.**

425g (15oz) icing sugar
4 balls stem ginger in syrup, drained and grated, plus 1–2 extra to decorate
1 medium egg white
Around 110g (4oz) each white chocolate and milk chocolate

Sing-a-long

'Oh,
I love to suck a humbug
Half a pound a week,
But it doesn't thrill me
Half as much
As ginger cheek to cheek.'

COFFEE CREAMS

My Coffee Creams are made with a secret ingredient – marshmallow – for extra unctuousness, then topped off with a pert, chocolate-coated coffee bean.

   In the 1970s Coffee Creams were found in a box of Milk Tray – usually left until last and then eaten by the dog along with the last of the Cadbury's Smash and your Bay City Rollers' jumper. I think you will find mine a vast improvement.

★ Fluff the marshmallows in a bowl and add ½ tablespoon of water. Microwave on High for 1 minute, if you are modern, or melt carefully in a pan on the hob. Stir to dissolve any little blobs of drowning marshmallows, bashing them with a wooden spoon if they resist death.
★ Add the icing sugar and coffee essence and mix together. If you are a Mary Queen, put your marigolds on; if you are butch, don't bother. Tip out onto a clean board and knead well to mix in the icing sugar – you may need an extra fairy sprinkling of icing sugar to stop it sticking.
★ Pick off walnut-sized knobs of the mixture and shape them into balls. Rub them together to make a chipolata shape and press one side down on the board so that it has a flat bottom. Leave them to dry on baking parchment for about 6 hours.
★ Temper the chocolate (see page 13). Put a wire cooling rack over a board or baking sheet. Use a chocolate dipping fork or table fork to plunge the coffee sweets into the chocolate. Lift out, let the excess chocolate dribble wantonly back into the bowl and set them on the rack. When you've covered all the coffee sweets, dip each coffee bean into the chocolate and set one on top of each sweet. Leave to set.

★ **Makes 18 retro creams**

★ **Take 30 minutes to make; plus overnight drying.**

50g (2oz) white
   marshmallows
125g (4½oz) icing sugar,
   plus extra for dusting
   (optional)
2 tsp Camp Coffee essence
   or 2 tsp cooled strong
   coffee
Dark chocolate, for
   tempering
18 chocolate-covered
   coffee beans (please
   see the end of this book
   for stockists)

GOOSEBERRY TRIFLE TRUFFLES

★ **Makes 11 sweet trifles**

★ **Take 30 minutes to make; plus 1 hour chilling and setting.**

White chocolate, for tempering
75g (3oz) gooseberries
1 tbsp elderflower cordial
40g (1 ½oz) white chocolate
40g (1 ½oz) fresh vanilla custard
1–2 traditional crunchy Amaretti biscuits, finely chopped
Gold lustre, for decadence

11-hole fluted cup chocolate mould (please see the end of this book for stockists)

I love these little truffles; made with elderflower cordial, gooseberries from my garden, a little vanilla custard and fluffy sponge all cuddled together in a white-chocolate cup. The first recipe for 'trifle' was published in England in 1596, in a book called *The Good Huswife's Jewell*, by Thomas Dawson.

★ Adjust your curlers. Temper the white chocolate (see page 13) and use a clean, grease-free brush, if you are the clean sort, or teaspoon to coat and line each of the fluted cups in the mould with the white chocolate. Any good housewife will understand the need for speed so work quickly otherwise the chocolate will cool and become too thick. Use a sharp knife or chocolate scraper or window squeegy to tidy up any bits around the chocolate shells, if you have no life at all. Scrape any white chocolate that you haven't used into a bowl and save to use again. Put the moulds in the fridge to set for around 20 minutes.

★ Meander out into the garden and pick some gooseberries. Supermarkets have lovely gardens. Put the goosegogs in a pan, add the cordial and 1 tablespoon of cold water. Bring to a gentle, giggling simmer and cook until the gooseberries are soft and start to burst. Cool a tad, then mercilessly whiz them in a mini blender, or squidge using a mortar and pestle to make a thick mush. Push through a plastic sieve into a bowl to make a purée. Toss the seeds and skin left behind into the bin.

★ Heat 5cm (2in) water in a pan. Slap a heatproof bowl on top of the pan, making sure the bottom of the bowl is not grazing the water. Using well practised housewifely skills, place the chocolate and custard in the bowl and warm through, gently stirring them until all the chocolate has melted. Take off the heat and stir in the gooseberry purée. Look at it longingly and whisper sweet nothings. Cool.

★ Remove the chocolate mould from the fridge and carefully upturn it onto a board so the fluted cups slide out like a Vaselined jumbo hotdog out of a drain pipe. Turn the fluted cups the right way up, then divide the gooseberry mixture evenly among them. Adorn with the crushed Amaretti biscuits and titillate with a little gold lustre. Chill for at least 30 minutes to set the gooseberry mixture.

Tip
Also included in The Good Huswife's Jewell you will find chapters on 'Foot massage for work-weary husbands', 'How not to be a clever wife', 'Bicarbonate of Soda — expert scrubbing techniques for ladies'.

SEASHELL CARAMELS

★ **Makes 20 seashell chocolates**

★ **Take 25 minutes to make; plus chilling and cooling time.**

Dark chocolate, for
    tempering
55ml (2fl oz) double cream
½ level tbsp dark
    muscovado sugar
15g (½oz) caster sugar
A good pinch of sea salt
    crystals (I use Maldon)
White chocolate, for
    tempering

Chocolate moulds with
    20 assorted seashells
    (please see the end of
    this book for stockists)

Mr G and I often take a trip to the South Coast with a little gas stove and a packet of sausages. I was sitting watching the sea as it furled its white fingers around my Crocs when the idea of popping, oozing, salted caramel inside a two-chocolate seashell came to me.

'I am quite brilliant,' says I, zipping up my cagoule.

'Harumph,' mumbles Mr G, flipping his sausage.

★ First up please temper the dark chocolate (see page 13) and use a brush or a teaspoon to coat and line the seashell moulds admirably. Do this quickly or suffer the consequences. Use a sharp knife or chocolate scraper tongue to tidy up any messy bits around the chocolate shells. Scrape any dark chocolate that you haven't used into a bowl and save it to use again, unlikely I know. Slide the moulds in the fridge to set for around 20 minutes – about the same time it takes to eat a tub of whelks washed down with Spar Cava.

★ To make the salted caramel, put the cream and dark muscovado sugar into a small, high-sided heatproof bowl or jar and rest it in a heatproof bowl of boiling water to warm gently, ensuring the water does not slop into the sugar and cream.

★ Pour the caster sugar into a small heavy-based pan and lodge on low to medium heat to dissolve the sugar, stirring it now and then until it is dark and golden. Peer at it anxiously like a seal watching a boat of tourists promising a sardine dinner disguised as a rounders bat.

P.T.O.

★ Whip the pan off the heat and slop in the warmed cream and muscovado – step away from the pan as it will as it will bubble up like a Geordie lass in a small Wonderbra. Once the initial bubbling subsides, grab a wooden spoon in there and stir furiously, faster, faster, to make a lovely caramel. Cool a wee bit, then stir in the salt.

★ When the caramel has cooled, whip the chocolate moulds out of the fridge and divide the caramel amongst the chocolate shells. Chill to achieve the firmness of Hector Harris the Scottish Girder.

★ Temper the white chocolate, as before. Spoon the chocolate over the caramel to cover. Chill again for 15 minutes – try a warm bath or a bit of telly. When hard, gently upturn the mould onto a board with a persuasive thumbing and release the chocolates.

★ Store in an airtight container in the fridge for up to 5 days.

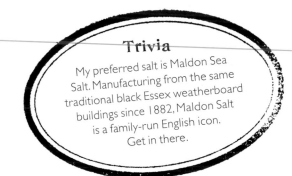

Trivia

My preferred salt is Maldon Sea Salt. Manufacturing from the same traditional black Essex weatherboard buildings since 1882, Maldon Salt is a family-run English icon. Get in there.

CHILLI AND LIME KISSES

Apparently Christopher Columbus discovered the chilli pepper on one of his travels; I can't remember where he was at the time, somewhere foreign, probably. To celebrate, natives honoured him with palm-leaf platters laden with these fiery, chocolate kisses filled with spicy chilli jam and a twist of lime.

★ Heat 5cm (2in) water in a pan. Whack a heatproof bowl on top of the pan, making sure the round bottom of the bowl is not touching the water. Delight the bowl by adding dark chocolate and cream and warming them languorously until melted. Take the pan off the heat.
★ Add the butter, lime zest, chilli and salt to the bowl and stir liberally. Set aside to cool a bit.
★ Temper the white chocolate (see page 13) and use a brush or a teaspoon to coat and line the lip moulds. Use a sharp knife or chocolate scraper to tidy up any sloppy bits around the chocolate shells. If you are so inclined, scrape any white chocolate that you haven't used into a bowl and save to use again. Put the moulds in the fridge to set for around 20 minutes. Turn a sheet, polish the door knob, race a pigeon.
★ Scoop up a little of the dark chocolate and chilli mixture with a teaspoon and use to fill each lip in the mould. Leave a gap of couple of millimetres at the top, otherwise there won't be enough space for the chocolate topping. Chill in the fridge for about 20 minutes.

★ **Makes 40 fiery lips**

★ **Take 40 minutes to make; plus chilling and setting time.**

50g (2oz) dark
   chocolate, finely
   chopped
2 tbsp double cream
10g (½oz) unsalted
   butter, chopped
Zest of ½ lime
⅛ tsp crushed chilli
   flakes, ground into
   a powder
A pinch of salt
White chocolate,
   for tempering

2 x 20 lips chocolate
moulds (please see
the end of this book
for stockists)

P.T.O.

He sailed from Spain in 1492...

He left on September...
forced to promise...
turn back...
days.

On t...
On one of...
now call W...
the Royal S...
to Cuba, an...
returning...
Santa M...

furth...
cove...
lan...
had...
make his posi...
or. The gover...
in as a prison...

fearin...
sent o...
Columb...
chains.

He was set free in 1502 to make a fourth voyage, but failed to find the passage to Asia for which he was seeking. He returned to Spain a disa... d man, too sick even to go to court, an... e died in poverty in the to... of Valla...

173

★ Temper some more white chocolate or use any that's left over from before (but you might need to add some more chocolate to it). Use a teaspoon to fill the moulds, covering all of the dark chocolate and chilli mixture. Chill again until set.

★ Take the chocolates out of the fridge and upturn onto a board – they should slip out easily – just like the lie you told about Bob and the banana. Any that are reluctant to disembark may require a persuasive twist of the mould to release them.

History Fact
It is widely accepted that Christopher Columbus had a busy year in 1492.

HOPE AND GREENWOOD

SPLENDID CONFECTIONERY

Fruit and Nut

CHAPTER TWO

LIME AND COCONUT TRUFFLES

★ **Makes 18 Calypso truffles**

★ **Take 20 minutes to make; plus chilling, overnight setting and 15 minutes to strap a broom handle between 2 kitchen chairs.**

50ml (2fl oz) double cream
100g (3½oz) white
    chocolate, chopped
60g (2½oz) desiccated
    coconut
Zest of 1 lime, juice of
    ½ lime
A pinch of salt
50g (2oz) unsalted butter,
    chopped

'I hold the record, darlink', says my best chum, Hans Rollo the Human Slinky, reaching for another of my tinglingly fresh Lime and Coconut Truffles, '*Calypso Limbo Dancer of the Decade*, sweetie – shimmied right under a burning broom handle without singeing my tassels'.

★ Heat 5cm (2in) water in a pan. Whack a heatproof bowl on top of the pan, making sure the bottom of the bowl is not touching the water. Grace the bowl with the cream and chocolate and warm to melt it, then stir together with kindness and humility.
★ Stir in 20g (¾oz) of the desiccated coconut along with the lime zest and juice, salt and butter. Cover and leave to set overnight.
★ Sprinkle the remaining 40g (1½oz) coconut in a dry frying pan and heat gently until toasted. Tip out onto a plate, down your nightie and into your slippers.
★ Take small teaspoons of the truffle mixture and roll it into balls. Roll each ball in the toasted coconut, then stick it on a piece of baking parchment. Chill again for at least 30 minutes until it is as firm as Hans Rollo's buttocks.

Celebrity Gossip
Hans Rollo performed with Larry Laslo – The Owl Man of Sheppey, Esther Dumas – Half Woman, Half Crab Stick, and Hortense Crawfish – the Naked Celebrity Escapologist.

AGEN PRUNES WITH BRANDY GANACHE

The Agen prune, a dried plum, is grown in the sun-kissed southwest of France. It gets its name from the port from which it is shipped all over the world – Agen. I have thumbed a wedge of deep and glorious dark chocolate and brandy ganache inside my yielding prune and smothered it with cocoa. Please excuse me while I wipe dribble off my typewriter.

★ Heat 5cm (2in) water in a pan. Pop a heatproof bowl on top of the pan, making sure the bottom of the bowl is not touching the water. The chocolate should be placed in the bowl to mingle joyously with the cream and brandy until melted together.

★ Use a sharp knife to split the vanilla pod lengthways. Run the tip of the knife down the length of the pod to extract the fragrant seeds. Add these to the bowl with the butter and stir all the ingredients together. Take the bowl off the heat and allow to cool.

★ Carefully push your thumb into a prune to make a well. Use a teaspoon to scoop up a little bit of ganache and roll it into a little round or a barrel, big enough to fill the prune. Repeat to use up all the prunes. Place on a 39 × 35cm (15¼ × 13¾in) baking sheet lined with baking parchment and chill for at least 30 minutes to set.

★ Dust each prune all over with cocoa and place them in petit four or mini-muffin cases.

★ **Makes 20 mouthwatering petit fours**

★ **Take 20 minutes to make; plus 1 hour cooling and chilling.**

50g (2oz) dark chocolate
1 tbsp double cream
1 tbsp French brandy
1 vanilla pod
25g (1oz) butter
20 Agen prunes
Cocoa powder, to dust

20 petit four or mini-muffin cases (please see the end of this book for stockists)

Trivia

An Agen prune can only come from Agen, just like a Melton Mowbray pork pie or Champagne, but unlike Newcastle Brown Ale, which is brewed in Gateshead – the nerve of those Geordies.

MANGO TRUFFLES

★ **Makes around
20 lucky truffles**

★ **Take around
45 minutes to make;
plus overnight freezing.**

½ small mango
100g (3½oz) white
  chocolate
2 tbsp double cream
25g (1oz) unsalted butter
175g (6oz) white
  chocolate, for tempering
1–2 dried mango pieces,
  chopped into small
  pieces
A little gold lustre (please
  see the end of this book
  for stockists)

The mango is considered by many to mean 'good luck'. In order to bring good fortune on yourself, simply prepare my fragrant Mango Truffles. Put on your lucky pulling pants, fashion a boob tube from the leaves of the mystical mango tree and do a snake dance on your kitchen table. Hark! Is that Big Dave from next door popping over to borrow a plunger?

★ Scoop about 75g (3oz) mango out of its skin. Whiz the flesh to a pulp in a mini food processor, or just bash it using a mestal and porter.
★ Heat 5cm (2in) water in a pan. Put a heatproof bowl on top of the pan; don't let the bottom of the bowl touch the water. Place the chocolate and cream in the bowl and melt slowly. Do not overheat or you will end up with a fudge island in a sea of melted butter.
★ Slowly stir in the butter and mango purée until combined and chill for 3–4 hours. Use a teaspoon to scoop up small amounts of the mixture and shape into balls. Open freeze on a baking sheet lined with baking parchment until hard. Quickly shape them into rounds, then transfer to a container, cover, then freeze overnight.
★ Temper the chocolate (see page 13). Use a round-headed dipping fork, or two forks, to dip each mango ball into the white chocolate. Toss to coat then lift out and place on a sheet of baking parchment. Use the fork to spike up the chocolate a bit. Put a piece of mango on top of each truffle and set aside for the chocolate to set, then chill. Tickle with gold lustre before serving.

Ahem
In the eighteenth and nineteenth centuries, South Asian cows were fed exclusively on mango leaves and the coveted yellow textile dye, 'Indian Yellow', was excreted in their cow lemonade. Not very Farrow and Ball is it, darling?

BLACKBERRY CRUMBLE CHOCOLATE

'Despite inclement weather,' declared Elizabeth Bonnet, 'my good sisters and I have plundered the hedgerows of Wetherfield Park and devised some uncommonly tasty Blackberry Crumble Chocolates.'

'Surely,' cried Mrs Bonnet, 'these remarkably agreeable treats will suffice to see my Lizzy settled at Mr Dandy's estate with £50 a year, a 63-inch plasma screen, and a cupboard full of Pop Tarts?'

★ Temper the milk chocolate (see page 13) and use a clean, grease-free brush or teaspoon to coat and line each of the fluted cups in the mould with the chocolate. You may wish to act hastily as the chocolate will set quickly. Use a chocolate scraper or a knife to scrape away any chocolate from the top of the mould. Scrape any chocolate that you haven't used into a bowl and save to use again. Put the moulds in the fridge to set for around 20 minutes – you may use the time to sew some spotted muslin or to pick out some gay ribbons for the Wetherfield Ball.

★ Put the blackberry jam and crème de cassis in a pan and heat gently. Stir together. Wander aimlessly to the window licking the spoon timidly. Is that Mr Dandy cantering across The Park? Gosh those breeches are a tad restricting.

★ **Makes 11 tolerable morsels**

★ **Take 20 minutes to make; plus chilling and setting time.**

Milk chocolate, for tempering
1 ½ tbsp blackberry jam
1 tbsp crème de cassis
40g (1 ½oz) white chocolate
1 tbsp double cream
1 vanilla pod
20g (¾oz) unsalted butter, chopped
1 sponge finger, crushed
1 tbsp flaked almonds, toasted and roughly chopped
A little icing sugar, to dust

11-hole fluted cup chocolate mould (please see the end of this book for stockists)

P.T.O.

★ Heat 5cm (2in) water in a pan. Pop a heatproof bowl on top of the pan, making sure the bottom of the bowl is not touching the water. Melt the chocolate and cream in the bowl, allowing yourself a fleeting moment to daydream of Mr Dandy and his clingy riding breeches.

★ Split the vanilla pod lengthways and run the tip of a knife down the pod to extract the seeds. Add them to the bowl with the butter and stir everything together. Resist the temptation to lick the spoon.

★ Remove the chocolate cups from the mould by upturning them gently onto a board. Set them the right way up, then divide the boozy jam mix equally among the cups. Dollop with the white chocolate ganache.

★ Mix the crushed sponge finger with the almonds and divide equally among the cups. Allow to set by chilling for at least 30 minutes, then dust with icing sugar. Let us hope that Mr Dandy finds them tolerable and handsome enough to tempt him.

ORANGE ROCHERS

Rocher is French for 'rock'. My Orange Rochers are chewy, crunchy rocks of almonds and orange peel coated with a dark bitter chocolate. I once won a fancy dress competition dressed as a plate of Ferrero Rocher by using a truck of Ferreros and a glue gun. I was very popular around one in the morning, as I recall, just as the vol-au-vents ran out.

★ Temper the dark chocolate (see page 13).
★ Tip the flaked almonds into a non-stick frying pan and heat gently for a couple of minutes until toasted and golden, tossing every now and then, if you are so inclined. Cool. Finely chop the orange peel.
★ Mix the flaked almonds and candied orange peel together in a bowl. Add the tempered chocolate and mix well, making sure the chocolate coats your nuts – and fruit.
★ Line a 39 x 35cm (¼ x 13¾in) baking sheet with baking parchment. Use a teaspoon to spoon little piles of the mixture onto the baking sheet. Chill for at least 30 minutes for the chocolate to set.

★ **Makes 8 rocks**

★ **Take 15 minutes to make; plus cooling and setting.**

50g (2oz) dark chocolate
25g (1oz) flaked almonds
25g (1oz) candied
    orange peel

Trivia
Ferrero also make Nutella – obvious when you know, isn't it?

STRAWBERRY AND CREAM LOLLIES

★ **Makes 4 life-
affirming lollies**

★ **Take 15 minutes to
make; plus setting time.**

Milk chocolate, for
    tempering
25g (1oz) white chocolate
About 12 freeze-dried
    strawberries

4 wooden lolly sticks
    (please see the end of
    this book for stockists)

I am pootling along the windy, sun-kissed lanes of Cornwall, my head scarf is doing an Isadora Duncan and bluebirds chirrup a joyous greeting overhead, when a sign for Strawberry Cream Tea tempts me off road. Ladies and gentlemen, here is a postcard-perfect Cornish tearoom with pixies riding on snails, tamed Baskerville Hounds frolicking in ponds of Ambrosia Creamed Rice and where Agatha Christie is supping cider from a wishing well made entirely of fudge. Then I wake up and remember it is bin day.

★ Temper the milk chocolate (see page 13).
★ Heat 5cm (2in) water in a pan. Place a heatproof bowl on top of the pan, making sure the bottom of the bowl is not touching the water. Slap the white chocolate in the bowl and allow it to melt slowly.
★ Line a 39 x 35cm (15¼ x 13¾in) baking sheet with baking parchment. Use a 6cm (2½in) round cutter, baked bean tin or mug to draw four circles spaced apart on the parchment, add a smiley face, then turn it over so the ink is underneath. Spoon a pool of milk chocolate onto each circle to fill each round. Place a lolly stick at the bottom of each, then spoon over a little more chocolate. When the chocolate dries the stick will be securely set, yes it will, honest injuns.
★ Decorate the lollies with three perfectly positioned dried strawberries, then use a teaspoon to carefully blob the white chocolate over the strawberries. Leave them to set, that is the rule.

HAZELNUT SANDWICHES

★ **Makes 20 sandwiches**

★ **Take 30 minutes to make; plus chilling time.**

For the marzipan paste
75g (3oz) ground almonds
50g (2oz) golden caster
   sugar
50g (2oz) golden icing
   sugar, sifted
Zest of ½ lemon
½ medium egg white

For the hazelnut filling
A little vegetable oil
25g (1oz) granulated
   sugar
25g (1oz) toasted
   hazelnuts
25g (1oz) milk chocolate,
   chopped

Deep in the Dark Wood, the Great Lord of the Green rose up to his full height, his fecund boughs of ripe hazelnuts rattling wildly.

'Squirrel Greenwood, do you dare defy the Great Lord of the Green? Has your mummy not sent you to find the secret recipe for my marzipan-rich, toasted hazelnut sandwiches?'

Squirrel Greenwood looked back over his shoulder gingerly.

'Stop gassin', man – I run dis ting! Yo' feel me bro, is it?'

And he skipped off to meet Susie Stoat for a game of doctors and nurses.

★ First make your marzipan. Put the ground almonds in a large bowl and add the sugar and icing sugar, la-la-la. Stir in the lemon zest and egg white and mix everything together, kneading well. Lovingly wrap the mixture in cling film, give it a little kiss, and chill for about 30 minutes.

★ Next up line a 39 x 35cm (15¼ x 13¾in) baking sheet with baking parchment and brush with oil. Hurl the sugar and hazelnuts in a pan. Heat very gently until the sugar has dissolved, stirring as you go with a wooden spoon. Cook until the sugar turns a dark golden joy – as soon as it does, quickly pour it onto the oiled parchment and leave it to set. When cool, whiz in a food processor until fine.

★ Heat 5cm (2in) water in a pan. Pop a heatproof bowl on top of the pan, making sure the bottom of the bowl is not touching the water. Place the chocolate in the bowl and warm to melt it – if you stir it, it will go thick and 'orrible.

★ When the chocolate has melted, add the nut mixture and stir together. Chill for 30 minutes.

★ Roll out the marzipan to a rough rectangle measuring around 19 x 16cm (7½ x 6½in). Trim the edges to make the tidiest rectangle you can muster. Keep the leftover bits to roll out again later.

★ Spread around two-thirds of the hazelnut filling over one half of the marzipan and put the other half on top. Squish it down and then cut the 'sandwiches' into small squares. Reroll the leftover marzipan, fill with the spread and cut into more squares.

★ Put the squares on a flameproof baking sheet and either pop it under a really hot grill for 30 seconds or blowtorch them *Alien*-style to to toast the top of each one.

SQUIRREL SCHOOL REPORT
Squirrel Greenwood is a spirited pupil, getting up to juvenile pranks with his peer group – Willy Weasel, Hengis Hedgehog and Conan the Curly. You will pleased to learn that matron is recovering from the cream horn incident.

MISS HOPE'S CHOCOLATE BOX FRUIT AND NUT

CARDAMOM AND PISTACHIO SHARDS

This combination of cardamom, pistachios, rose syrup and milk chocolate is inspired by the Greek pastry baklava. Cardamom makes nearly anything taste better and I love the flavour of roses. My fragrant shards are as sweetly perfumed as Hebe, the Greek goddess of youth and cupbearer of the gods. Listen to her giggling as she pours the secret of eternal youth, Botox, from a golden pitcher.

★ Heat 5cm (2in) water in a pan. Plop a heatproof bowl on top of the pan, don't let the bottom of the bowl touch the water or the chocolate will burn. Place the milk chocolate in the bowl and gently warm it to melt. Add the butter, rose syrup and salt and stir until the butter has melted. Sniff generously. Remove the bowl from the heat and let it cool a bit.

★ Bash the cardamon pods with a rolling pin or in a mestle and portar, thus removing their shells. Bin the shells in one swift motion, and then grind down the remaining black seeds to make a fine powder.

★ Stir the cardamom and about three-quarters of the chopped pistachios into the chocolate and mix with gusto. Pour onto a 39 x 35cm (15¼ x 13¾in) baking sheet lined with baking parchment and scatter the remaining pistachios over. Leave in a cool place overnight to set. Once set, snap into uneven shards, you devil.

★ **Makes about 8 shards of eternal youth**

★ **Take 20 minutes to make; plus overnight setting.**

300g (11oz) good-quality milk chocolate, broken into small bits
25g (1oz) unsalted butter
½ tsp rose syrup
A generous pinch of salt
6 green cardamon pods
50g (2oz) pistachios, finely chopped

Culinary Tip
Please do use rose syrup, not rosewater, as rosewater is too watery. Or try a rose liqueur such as Briottet Liqueur de Rose, which you can also mix with champagne.

PEANUT BUTTERFLIES

Now, you know I am very fond of peanut butter, I have told you a thousand times – have you forgotten already? Please try to keep up. Here is a revelation: little milk chocolate butterflies filled with oozy, salty, peanut butter gloop. Make them, eat them, take a satisfied nap in a pot of sunny geraniums.

★ Temper the chocolate (see page 13) and use an unsullied, grease-free brush or teaspoon to coat and line each of the butterfly holes in the mould with the chocolate. Do this quickly otherwise the chocolate will cool and become too thick to work with – like Mavis in accounts. Use a spatula to scrape away any chocolate from the top of the mould. Scrape any chocolate that you haven't used into a bowl and save to use again. Put the moulds in the fridge to set for around 20 minutes.
★ Put the peanut butter, cream and sugar in a pan and heat gently, allowing the peanut butter to melt. Stir together and sing a little tune – la-la-la. Spoon the mixture into the set chocolate butterflies and level the tops of each one. Chill to allow the mixture to firm up.
★ Take the mould out of the fridge and allow it to come up to room temperature. Temper the remaining milk chocolate, or use the leftover tempered chocolate (you might need to add some more), and spoon over the peanut butter cream to cover. Chill for 30 minutes to set. Gently upturn onto a board and they should easily slide out like a bendy bus from a junction.

★ **Makes 9 flutterbies**

★ **Take about 30 minutes to make; plus 1 hour chilling.**

Milk chocolate, for
    tempering
50g (2oz) smooth peanut
    butter
10g (½oz) double cream
25g (1oz) soft light
    brown sugar

9-hole butterfly chocolate
    mould (please see the
    end of this book for
    stockists)

DATES FOR YOUR DIARY
The Good News is that 24 January is National Peanut Butter Day in the USA; the Bad News is that on 2 November they celebrate National Deviled Egg Day.

COFFEE WALNUT WHIPS

★ **Makes 11 gloopy whips**

★ **Take around 30 minutes to make; plus 1 hour chilling and overnight setting.**

Milk chocolate, for tempering
2 tbsp Camp Coffee essence
½ tbsp soft light brown sugar
50g (2oz) milk chocolate, chopped
11 walnuts

11-hole fluted cup chocolate mould (please see the end of this book for stockists)

Sweet Trivia
The Camp Coffee label portrays Major General Sir Hector Macdonald who, to the horror of his wife and children, shot himself when his camp tendencies were made public.

Whatever happened to the Coffee Walnut Whip? Whatever happened to the Walnut Whip that had two walnuts? Here is a rather grown-up version of the walnut whip, made using a gooey, dairy-free coffee filling. If you are like me, then you will, without shame, bite off the walnut then stick your tongue in and wiggle it about.

★ Temper the milk chocolate (see page 13) and use a clean, grease-free brush or teaspoon to coat and line each of the fluted cups in the mould. You need to do this faster than a ferret up a trouser leg or the chocolate will go thick and be rendered useless. Use a spatula to scrape away any chocolate from the top of the mould. Scrape any chocolate that you haven't used into a bowl and save to use again. Put the moulds in the fridge to set for around 20 minutes.
★ Put the coffee essence in a measuring jug and add enough cold water to make it up to 50ml (2fl oz). Pour into a pan, add the sugar and bring to the boil. Simmer for 1 minute.
★ Put the chopped milk chocolate in a bowl and splosh the coffee liquid over. Stir well and leave until cold.
★ Take the mould out of the fridge. Spoon the chocolate and coffee mixture into the mould and leave to set overnight.
★ Temper the remaining milk chocolate, or use the tempered chocolate left over from earlier (you might need to add some more chocolate), and using a teaspoon spoon it over the ganache to cover. Crown with a walnut. Chill for at least 30 minutes until set, then carefully upturn the mould onto a board to release the walnut whips.

MIXED HIGH-CLASS CHOCOLATES AND FINEST AMERICAN, SWISS AND
FRENCH SPECIALITIES. (See Chapter XI.)

No. 1.—Piped Truffle Chocolates.
No. 2.—Fruit Cream Bon-bons, decorated.
No. 3.—Finest Assorted Bon-bons, decorated, and
Parisian Creams.

No. 4.—Marzipan Cream Chocolates, decorated,
various shapes and flavours (see Chapter V).
No. 5.—Chocolates made in Block Tin Moulds, filled
with finest Creams and Pastes (see Chapter XV).
No. 6.—Fondant Cream Chocolates, various flavours.

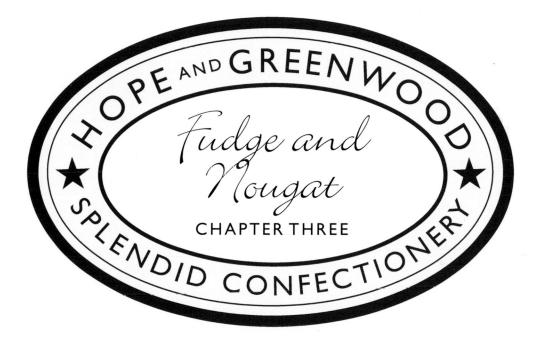

HOPE AND GREENWOOD

SPLENDID CONFECTIONERY

Fudge and Nougat

CHAPTER THREE

BLACK FOREST FUDGE

★ **Makes 49 squares
made in heaven**

★ **Take around
30 minutes to make;
plus cooling and
overnight chilling.**

40g (1½oz) unsalted
    butter, plus extra
    to grease
75g (3oz) dark glacé
    cherries (I used
    Billington's)
500g (1lb 2oz) golden
    caster sugar
275ml (10fl oz) double
    cream
75g (3oz) dark
    chocolate, grated
50g (2oz) white
    chocolate, grated

BLACK
FOREST DYNASTY
Helga and Johannes
also produced three
sons: Ritter, Oetker (who
became a famous
doctor) and Vorsprung
Durch Technik.

Once upon a time there was a master baker called Johannes.
Johannes lived in the Black Forest where he gathered berries
to make his famous Black Forest Gateau. One day he fell in
love with a comely dairy maid called Helga. Their marriage
produced this recipe for the creamiest chocolatey fudge,
studded with rich sticky cherries.

★ Generously butter a 17cm (6¾in) square tin and line it with
baking parchment, less than a turkey buttering, more than a slimmer's
sandwich. Cut 50g (2oz) of the sticky cherries in half, then quarter
the remaining fruits.
★ Put the sugar, cream and butter in a large, heavy-bottomed (I used
a deep 24cm (9½in) diameter pan) pan with 3 tablespoons of water.
Please heat gently for 5–10 minutes to dissolve the sugar. Thank you.
★ Pop a sugar thermometer in the pan and bring the liquid up to the
boil. Boil until the thermometer reaches 113°C (235°F).
★ Take the pan off the heat and pour around a third of the mixture
into a metal bowl. Add the dark chocolate to the remaining mixture
in the pan and the white chocolate to the metal bowl. Stir each with
separate spoons until they begin to thicken.
★ Now for the fun bit. Pour the dark chocolate into the square tin.
Sprinkle over the quartered cherries. Spoon over the white chocolate,
then drag a skewer through the mixture to create swirls all over.
★ Dot the halved cherries over the top, allow to cool, then chill
overnight until set. Remove from the tin and cut into squares.

PENUCHE

★ **Makes 34 fingers of fudge**

★ **Take about 1 hour 15 minutes to make; including cooling.**

40g (1½oz) unsalted butter, chopped, plus extra to grease
500g (1lb 2oz) light soft brown sugar
225ml (8fl oz) full-fat milk
A good pinch of salt
1 tsp vanilla extract
50g (2oz) dark chocolate

Penuche (pronounced *puh-noo-chee*) is part fudge, part candy. What distinguishes it from 'normal' fudge is the caramelised brown sugar that gives the penuche its beautiful colour; in fact it is not unlike the Finger of Fudge. So, if you fancy a change from the paler, British style of fudge, this is for you – made with soft brown sugar, dark chocolate and vanilla. If you are looking for a more radical change I have no objection, so long as you don't stretch my shoes.

★ Generously butter a 17cm (6¾in) square tin and line with baking parchment.
★ Put the sugar, milk and salt in a large, heavy-bottomed pan (I used a deep 24cm (9½in) diameter pan). Heat gently for around 3–5 minutes to dissolve the sugar. Pop a sugar thermometer into the pan, bring the mixture up to the boil and continue to cook, stirring all the time, until the temperature reaches 113°C (235°F).
★ Take the pan off the heat and dot over the chopped butter. Set aside for 30–45 minutes for the butter to melt and the mixture to cool. It's cool enough to beat together when you can comfortably hold your hand on the bottom of the pan.
★ When the mixture has cooled, add the vanilla extract and stir everything together. You'll need to work the butter in; keep at it, as it will eventually blend into the mixture. Continue to beat just until the mixture loses its gloss. Just think of your mother-in-law and how she watches you over the top of her glasses – not quite good enough, are you?

★ Quickly pour the fudge into the prepared tin and set aside until firm.

★ Heat 5cm (2in) water in a pan. Pop a heatproof bowl on top of the pan, making sure the bottom of the bowl is not touching the water. Place the chocolate in the bowl and allow it to melt slowly. Drizzle it lovingly over the fudge then set it aside to dry.

★ Take the fudge out of the tin, plonk it on a board, then cut it in half and cut across into 1cm (½in) fingers.

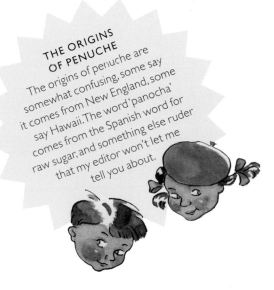

THE ORIGINS OF PENUCHE

The origins of penuche are somewhat confusing, some say it comes from New England, some say Hawaii. The word 'panocha' comes from the Spanish word for raw sugar, and something else ruder that my editor won't let me tell you about.

CHOCOLATE SORT-OF-NO-COOK FUDGE

This fudge is absolutely perfect if you are just not in the mood for thermometers and all that gubbins. It's also a cracking recipe if you have keen little chefs. There is some heating involved but with a little supervision they will find the stirring bit fun. Feel free to add your own favourite ingredients. Here I've used Smarties, because everyone likes them and they have no artificial colours or flavourings.

★ Generously butter a 17cm (6¾in) square tin and line with baking parchment.

★ Heat 5cm (2in) water in a pan. Pop a heatproof bowl on top of the pan, making sure the bottom of the bowl is not touching the water. Add the two types of chocolate, the butter, condensed milk and vanilla extract to the bowl.

★ Reduce the heat to the lowest setting and allow the chocolate and butter to melt.

★ Take the pan off the heat and have fun stirring all the ingredients together. Please be careful, you nana, the bowl is hot.

★ Pour into the prepared tin and scatter over the Smarties, pushing them gallantly into the fudge so that they stick. Cool, then chill overnight.

★ Remove from the fridge, cut into squares and get stuck in.

★ **Makes 49 jolly pieces**

★ **Take around 15 minutes to make; plus chilling – much less time than you spend on the phone to the Ikea helpline.**

60g (2½oz) unsalted butter, chopped, plus extra to grease
125g (4½oz) milk chocolate, chopped
125g (4½oz) dark chocolate, chopped
200g can sweetened condensed milk (NOT evaporated milk)
1 tsp vanilla extract
1 tube of Smarties

OTHER INGREDIENTS YOUR LITTLE CHEFS MAY WISH TO TRY: Play Doh, hair bobbles, Nan's best hat, Snuffles the rabbit, My Little Pony and cat food.

WHITE CHOCOLATE AND ROSEMARY NOUGAT

★ **Makes around 49 love chunks**

★ **Take 40 minutes to make; plus overnight setting, plus 3 days to create a 6-foot papier maché seashell.**

Tin foil and rice paper
   to line the tin
A dribble of vegetable oil
400g (14oz) caster sugar
100ml (3½fl oz) runny
   honey
210ml (7fl oz) liquid
   glucose
2 large egg whites,
   at room temperature
40g (1½oz) dried
   raspberries
75g (3oz) shelled
   pistachios, toasted
75g (3oz) blanched
   almonds, toasted
100g (3½oz) white
   chocolate, chopped into
   chunks then frozen

The word 'rosemary' comes from the Greek words *Ros Marinus*, meaning 'Dew of the Sea', tendrils of which were twirled around Aphrodite's neck when she rose from the ocean in a Botticelli seashell, like you do. Legend has it that she was after a bit of my utterly fabulous white honeyed nougat with candied peel, pistachios, almonds, dried raspberries and rosemary. Being the Goddess of Love can leave one feeling terribly peckish.

★ Line the base and sides of a 20cm (8in) square tin with tin foil and brush all over with a little vegetable oil, in a jaunty Picasso manner. Line the base with rice paper.

★ Put the sugar, honey and liquid glucose in a large heavy-bottomed pan (I used a deep 24cm (9½in) diameter pan) with 2 tablespoons cold water. Heat gently to dissolve the sugar. Place a sugar thermometer in the pan and bring the mixture to the boil. Allow it to bubble until the temperature reaches 125°C (257°F).

★ Meanwhile, put the egg whites in the bowl of a freestanding mixer and whisk them until stiff peaks form, but taking care not to over-thwack them.

★ When the syrup reaches 125°C (257°F) you need to work quickly. Ready? Start the beaters, running on a low to medium setting, then whip out the sugar thermometer and pour half of the syrup in a steady stream onto the egg white and continue to beat. Go! Go! Go!

★ Return the pan with the remaining syrup to the heat, pop the thermometer back in and continue to cook until the temperature reaches 157°C (315°F). The mixture should be a beauticious, dark caramel colour. Pour this mixture into the food mixer, super slowly – it will froth up to the top of the mixing bowl like a mad dog on a hot day. Mix on a moderate speed for a few minutes to incorporate all the syrup and until the mixture decreases in volume. Turn off the mixer – obviously.

★ Fold in the raspberries, toasted nuts, white chocolate, peel and thyme or rosemary. Pour the mixture into the prepared tin, pressing it down evenly, then put two sheets of rice paper on top. Chill overnight until firm. Cut the nougat into pieces and dance around the coffee table in your pants.

75g (3oz) whole candied orange peel, chopped into small pieces
2 small sprigs of thyme or rosemary

FYI
Aphrodite was married to an ugly bloke but made up for it by carrying on with endless bits of rough. She was a bit of a hussy really.

MALTED NOUGAT

★ **Makes 25 sticky pieces**

★ **Take 30 minutes to make; plus overnight setting.**

A dribble of vegetable oil
Tin foil and rice paper to
   line the tin
400g (14oz) caster sugar
100ml (3½fl oz) clear
   honey
210ml (7fl oz) liquid
   glucose
2 large egg whites, at
   room temperature
50g (2oz) dark chocolate,
   melted and cooled
40g (1½oz) chocolate
   Ovaltine powder
A good pinch of salt
75g (3oz) Maltesers
   (plus another 75g (3oz)
   for you to eat, because
   you know you will)

It is time for bed chez Greenwood; I am wearing my new PJs, they are warm and comforting, my hot water bottle is filled, steaming water bubbling over its neck with excitement. A warm mug of malty, chocolate Ovaltine beckons. The very next morning I set to and create this soft and yielding nougat studded with Maltesers. It smells like my childhood – without the Plastercine and Elnett.

★ Line a 17cm (6¾in) square tin with tin foil and brush all over with a little vegetable oil. Line the base with rice paper.

★ Put the sugar, honey and liquid glucose in a large heavy-bottomed pan (I used a deep 24cm (9½in) diameter pan) with 2 tablespoons cold water. Heat gently to dissolve the sugar. Pop a sugar thermometer in the pan and bring the mixture to the boil. Allow to bubble until the temperature reaches 125°C (257°F).

★ Meanwhile, put the egg whites in the bowl of a freestanding mixer and whisk until stiff peaks form, taking care not to overbeat.

★ When the syrup reaches 125°C (257°F) you need to work quickly. Start the beaters, running on a low to medium setting, then whip out the sugar thermometer and pour half of the syrup in a steady stream onto the egg white and continue to beat – it is neither a carpet nor a Tom Brown spanking.

P.T.O.

★ Return the pan with the remaining syrup to the heat, pop the thermometer back in and continue to cook until the temperature reaches 157°C (315°F). The mixture should be a dark caramel colour. Pour this mixture into the food mixer, slowly as you go. It will froth up to the top of the mixing bowl. Mix on a moderate speed for a few minutes to incorporate all the syrup. The mixture will thin down after a minute or so.

★ Add the chocolate and Ovaltine powder with the salt and continue to mix until these are both incorporated – the mixture will turn from caramel to a rich nutty brown.

★ Pour the mixture into the prepared tin, scatter over half the Maltesers, then chop some and halve the remainder and scatter them over the top. Cool, then leave to set overnight. Cut into squares before serving. Give yourself a round of applause – that was quite a tricky one.

Maltesers® **Trivia**

Forrest E. Mars created Maltesers® in 1936. They are so bubbly brilliant that the Mars family business is still making them in the same factory in Slough today, over 70 years later. In 2007 Mars made over 10 billion Malteser balls – enough to lasso the world over 3.7 times.

HONEY AND ALMOND WHITE CHOCOLATE FUDGE

Last night I discovered two bears on my sofa surrounded by the remnants of my White Chocolate Fudge. Honestly, bears take such liberties; using my shampoo, leaving their wet towels on the floor, playing loud music, girls coming and going at all hours. They treat this place like a hotel.

★ Generously butter a 17cm (6¾in) square tin and line with baking parchment. Plonk the butter, sugar, cream and honey in a large heavy-bottomed pan (I used a deep 24cm (9½in) diameter pan). Heat gently and stir the mixture together. You must make sure all the sugar has dissolved, so test it by dipping the back of a teaspoon into the mixture and running your finger or tongue down it. Keep heating and stirring on a gentle heat if any grains remain.

★ As soon as all the sugar has dissolved, turn up the heat to medium until you get a rolling boil. Continue to stir the mixture for about 15 minutes. It will metamorphose from looking a bit like a white sauce to the beautiful colour of thick-set honey.

★ Take the pan off the heat. If you are astute you will notice the mixture still bubbling up now; it looks delicious but don't, even if you are wilful, be tempted to stick any part of your anatomy in it. Stir in the chocolate, almonds and apricots. Beat well for 5–10 minutes until the mixture loses its shine and gloss and becomes thick and pasty.

★ Spoon into the prepared tin and smooth over. Leave to cool, then chill to set. Remove the fudge from the tin, cut into squares and dance a dance with waggly arms, like a spider-monkey-crab-beast.

★ **Makes 50 honeyed pieces; 40 to serve and 10 to eat**

★ **Take a good 40 minutes of your time.**

25g (1oz) unsalted butter, plus extra to grease
400g (14oz) caster sugar
300ml (½ pint) double cream
2 tsp clear honey
25g (1oz) white chocolate, roughly chopped
50g (2oz) whole almonds, toasted and roughly chopped
50g (2oz) ready-to-eat dried apricots, roughly chopped

NOUGAT CLUSTERS

In this really simple but delightful recipe, Rice Krispies®, creamy milk chocolate, sour cherries, pecans and white nougat are all clustered together in chewy harmony. They are almost as simple as Simple Simon and his Dancing Teeth.

★ Put the nougat on a freezerproof plate and and slip it into the freezer. Line a board with baking parchment.
★ Temper the chocolate (see page 13).
★ Make 8 dainty piles of the remaining ingredients on a board, dividing the Rice Krispies equally among them so no one gets jealous.
★ When the chocolate is tempered, remove the nougat from the freezer and pop a piece onto each Krispie pile.
★ Balance a pile of the ingredients on a dessertspoon and scoop it into the chocolate, making sure all the ingredients are covered. Place the chocolatey cluster on the parchment. Repeat to cover all the piles. Towards the end, you may need to dribble any naked bits the chocolate hasn't covered with the chocolate left over in the bowl.
★ Allow to set, then temper the white chocolate. Dip a balloon whisk into the white chocolate and drizzle it all over the clusters. Enjoy!

★ **Makes 8 whoppers**

★ **Take 15 minutes to make; plus setting time.**

8 pieces white nougat
Good-quality milk
   chocolate, for tempering
8 dried soured cherries
8 whole pecan nuts
2 tbsp Rice Krispies
White chocolate, for
   tempering

Rice Krispie®
Trivia
'Oh, The words 'Snap! Crackle and Pop!' are the sounds made by the Krispies when they come into contact with milk. In other countries they sound like this:

Dutch: 'Pif! Paf! Pof!'
Gujarati: 'Maro! Mathu! Maar!'
Canadian French: 'Cric! Crac! Croc!'
German: 'Knisper! Knasper! Knusper!'
Romanian: 'Clampanitul! Auzi! Pop!'
Afrikaans: 'Knap! Knetter! Knak!'

Now, isn't your
life enriched?

MARSHMALLOW FUDGE FONDUE

★ **Makes 4 blast-from-the-past servings**

★ **Take about 10 minutes.**

250g (9oz) milk chocolate, broken into pieces
4 squares Honey and Almond White Chocolate Fudge (see page 77) or 4 pieces of Hope and Greenwood fudge
150ml (¼ pint) double cream
150ml (¼ pint) full-fat milk
4 Hope and Greenwood marshmallows (around 50g/2oz)
Baileys or Rum (optional)

To dip in . . .
Hope and Greenwood marshmallows
Slices of peaches and nectarines
Whole strawberries
Cherry earrings
Boudoir biscuits

The word 'fondue' comes from the French verb *fonder* – to melt. My fondue is a warm embrace of chocolate, fudge and marshmallows, into which you can stick anything that takes your fancy; I suggest cherries and strawberries, for safety reasons. The fondue was the height of sophistication in the 1970s, washed down with a glass of Riesling and a blast of John Denver's 'Leaving on a Jet Plane'.

★ Put the chocolate in a pan with the fudge. Pour in the cream and milk and add the marshmallows. Really, there is no hope for your thighs at this point. Place the pan over a gentle heat and allow the chocolate to melt slowly.

★ Once all the chocolate has melted, stir everything together with a wooden spoon. Lick the spoon a couple of times, put it back into the mixture and lick it again just in case you get hungry later. Pour the melted mixture into a bowl. Select your finest plate and arrange the marshmallows, fruit and Boudoir biscuits frivolously.

★ If you are feeling frisky you could add a sploosh of Baileys or Rum.

LEMON AND BLUEBERRY NOUGAT

There is very little in this life nicer than my silken nougat – laden with blueberries and crystallised lemon peel. This is a white, Torrone-style nougat, chewy rather than hard and sandwiched between sheets of rice paper. Some may consider Colin Firth licking champagne from their navel a nicer treat than my nougat; to you I say, 'weirdo celebrity fantasist'.*

★ Line the base of a 17cm (6¾in) square tin with rice paper, allowing it to come up the sides.
★ Put the sugar, honey and liquid glucose in a large heavy-bottomed pan (I used a deep 24cm (9½in) diameter pan) with 125ml (4½fl oz) cold water. Heat gently to dissolve the sugar. Pop a sugar thermometer in the pan and bring the mixture to the boil. Allow it to bubble until the temperature reaches 125°C (257°F).
★ Meanwhile, put the egg whites in the bowl of a freestanding mixer and whisk until stiff peaks form, taking care not to overbeat.
★ When the syrup reaches 125°C (257°F) you need to work quickly. Start the beaters, running on a low to medium setting, then whip out the sugar thermometer and pour half of the syrup in a steady stream onto the egg white and continue to beat.

★ **Makes 25 silken pieces**

★ **Take 40 minutes to make; plus overnight chilling.**

Rice paper
400g (14oz) caster sugar
100ml (3½fl oz) clear honey
210ml (7fl oz) liquid glucose
2 large egg whites, at room temperature
A pinch of salt
50g (2oz) candied lemon peel, chopped
75g (3oz) flaked almonds, toasted
75g (3oz) dried blueberries
40g (1½oz) white chocolate chips
A handful of fresh blueberries, to scatter over the top

P.T.O.

★ Return the pan with the remaining syrup to the heat, pop the thermometer back in and continue to cook until the temperature reaches 157°C (315°F). The mixture should be a dark caramel colour. Pour this mixture into the food mixer, slowly; it will froth up to the top of the mixing bowl. Add the salt. Mix on a moderate speed for a few minutes to incorporate all the syrup. Now you can turn the mixer off.
★ Fold in the candied peel, most of the almonds and the dried blueberries then pour into the tin. Sprinkle over the white chocolate chips with the remaining almonds and the fresh blueberries and leave to cool. Leave to set overnight before cutting into squares.

Dear Mr Firth,
You are cordially invited to lick champagne from my navel on 21 September at 8pm. Dress optional.
Miss WCF (Weirdo Celebrity Fantasist)

MAPLE AND PECAN FUDGE

This recipe for rich creamy fudge, succulent with maple syrup and encrusted with pecans and smooth milk chocolate, was given to me by my chum Fearless Freddie, the entrepreneurial monkey and owner of the Fearless Freddie Food Empire. Freddie loves nuts and is responsible for creating iconic household brands such as the Go Bananas Bar and Monkey Magic Cereal.

★ Generously butter a 17cm (6¾in) square tin and line with baking parchment. Ease the butter into a large heavy-bottomed pan (I used a deep 24cm (9½in) diameter pan) and add the sugar. Add the evaporated milk, cream and maple syrup. Heat gently, stir the ingredients into a delicious mess making sure that the sugar has dissolved – this will take 3–5 minutes, so make yourself comfortable.
★ Pop a sugar thermometer in the pan and increase the heat until the mixture is boiling, stirring the mixture all the time with a wooden spoon. Heat until the temperature reaches 113°C (235°F).
★ Take the pan off the heat and plonk in the pecans. Stir them in then beat the mixture really hard, just until it starts to lose its gloss and become a bit paler – it should still be pourable at this point, *ipso facto* pour into the prepared tin.
★ Sprinkle the chocolate over the fudge mixture, then set aside to cool. When cool, remove the fudge from the tin and cut into squares.

★ **Makes 49 encrusted pieces**

★ **Take about 30 minutes to make; plus cooling time.**

25g (1oz) unsalted butter, plus extra to grease
300g (11oz) light soft brown sugar
170g can evaporated milk
100ml (3½fl oz) double cream
4 tbsp maple syrup
50g (2oz) pecans
50g (2oz) milk chocolate, chopped or grated

Coming Soon

'Go Nuts!' New to Discover It! channel, Fearless Freddie puts six would-be entrepreneurs through their paces in the urban jungle. Next week: How many macadamias can they fit into a Honda?

HOPE AND GREENWOOD

SPLENDID CONFECTIONERY

Tipples

CHAPTER FOUR

BRANDY ALMOND DATES

★ **Makes around 18 'Is it Christmas?' dates**

★ **Take around 40 minutes to make; plus drying time.**

40g (1½oz) pine nuts
40g (1½oz) ground almonds
25g (1oz) golden caster sugar
½ tsp ground cinnamon
1 tbsp brandy
Splash of rosewater
About 18 Medjool dates
50g (2oz) dark chocolate, broken into pieces

Say 'hello' to my plump dates stuffed with ground almonds and brandy, splashed with rosewater and dribbled with dark chocolate. The best date to use is the Medjool date, the 'king of dates' or 'crown jewel of dates', which is large and extremely sweet. Dates are good for everything, including tummy aches, sore throats and fever – and they can even be used as a hangover cure.

★ Put the pine nuts in a small food blender and whiz until finely ground. Don't over chop otherwise the nuts will become greasy. Failing that, chop them for about 3 hours until fine and you have repetitive strain injury.

★ Whack them into a bowl with the ground almonds, sugar and cinnamon. Stir in the brandy, rosewater and about 1 teaspoon of water. Mix well – oh, it is the embodiment of sleigh bells and snow.

★ Use a sharp knife to cut along the length of each date. Take out the stones, then thumb the nut mixture into your date. Put them somewhere sensible to firm up; a sloppy date is no good to anyone.

★ Heat 5cm (2in) water in a pan. Put a heatproof bowl on top of the pan, making sure the bottom of the bowl is not touching the water. Place the chocolate in the bowl and allow it to melt slowly.

★ Use a teaspoon to drizzle the chocolate over the dates in a zig-zaggy manner and then let the chocolate dry for 20 minutes or so, if you can wait that long.

Top Tip
Hot dates are probably the most desirable of all dates.

RUM AND RAISIN TRUFFLES

★ **Makes 22 scurvilicious truffles**

★ **Take 30 minutes to make; plus 4 hours soaking and time to firm up.**

50ml (2fl oz) rum
50g (2oz) raisins
100g (3½oz) dark chocolate
2 tbsp double cream
75g (3oz) Madeira cake, crumbled
Chocolate sprinkles, such as vermicelli or flakes

I have the bon viveur pirate Cap'n Broderick Leadfoot to thank for these rich, dark chocolate Rum and Raisin Truffles. Cap'n Rick was famous for his flamboyant dress sense, often commanding his ship, the *Thunder of Atlantis*, in a tiara, sometimes sitting down to dinner for all the world attired as a French maid. Nonetheless, his truffles are truly scurvilicious and well worth trying.

★ Sploosh the rum in a pan and throw in the raisins. Bring up to the boil and simmer for 1–2 minutes. Hide it in a cool place for about 4 hours. Perhaps swing in a hammock, take a bath, a nap, or a bottle of sherry down the garden.

★ Put the raisins in a small blender with any rum they haven't absorbed and whiz to make a purée. Or whack them in a mortar and bash them senseless.

★ Heat 5cm (2in) water in a pan. Pop a heatproof bowl on top of the pan, making sure the bottom of the bowl is not touching the water. Place the chocolate in the bowl with the cream and heat to allow the chocolate to melt happily. Stir in the rum purée and the pieces of Madeira cake. Stir everything together, tasting regularly.

★ Take teaspoonfuls of the mixture and roll them into balls. Sprinkle the vermicelli and flakes into two separate shallow dishes. Roll half of the truffles in each. Set aside until firm as a pirate's stump.

WHERE IS HE NOW?
Tragically, Cap'n Rick went mad, succumbing to naked deck games such as Hang the Monkey and Dead Man's Trouser.

WHISKY MAC FONDANTS

Angry farmer Fred Rant from Shittleheugh Farm recently sent me this recipe for his warming ginger fondants infused with a stiff whisky and sticky ginger wine. 'Lived on't moors all me life,' he bellowed, 'sewed me own head back on wi' fishing wire after accident with scythe and walked twenty foower miles to the shops in't blizzard for ingredients. Aye, there be no shandy swilling, namby pamby southerners round these parts.'

★ Sift the icing sugar into a bowl and add the grated ginger. Watch your fingers, and remember grating is woman's work. In a separate clean bowl, beat the egg white until just frothy, man, and add it to the icing sugar with the ginger wine and whisky. Stir everything together.
★ Make the sweet fondant by kneading the mixture until smooth and all the icing sugar has been sucked up.
★ Roll out the mixture between two pieces of baking parchment to a thickness of 3mm (just under ⅛in), then cut into diamonds. Leave on baking parchment to dry out overnight while you sober up.
★ Chop the extra stem ginger for decorating into slivers. Temper the chocolate (see page 13). Using a dipping fork, if you are posh, or two ordinary forks, if you are a peasant, dip each ginger cream into the chocolate. Place the fondants onto a sheet of baking parchment and decorate each with a piece of ginger. Leave to set while you are in the pub.

★ **Makes 18 fiery diamonds**

★ **Take 40 minutes to make; plus overnight setting.**

125g (4½oz) unrefined icing sugar
1 ball stem ginger in syrup, drained and grated, plus ½ ball to decorate
Around 1 tbsp egg white
½ tsp ginger wine
½ tsp whisky
Dark chocolate, for tempering

DEVON STRAWBERRY TRUFFLES

As a little homage to the Devonshire Tea, my truffles are filled with a milk chocolate, strawberry ganache and covered in white chocolate. If you've not tried a Devonshire Tea, please do pop into my house any day between 3pm and 5pm and I will rustle up some warm scones, clotted cream and strawberry jam. How much love can one woman give?

★ Heat 5cm (2in) water in a pan. Pop a heatproof bowl on top of the pan, making sure the bottom of the bowl is not touching the water. Place the chocolate and cream in the bowl and let the chocolate melt.

★ Remove from the heat, add the butter and liqueur to the bowl and stir. A little whisk is really handy to beat everything together here; you may be tempted to use your tongue, but remember, Father Christmas is watching. Spoon into a sealable container and chill overnight to set.

★ Line a 39 × 35cm (15¼ × 13¾in) baking sheet with baking parchment. Take teaspoons of the mixture and roll it into balls. Place them on the baking sheet and freeze for at least 4 hours until as hard as Big Bunty the Muscleman's Daughter.

★ Temper the white chocolate (see page 13). Use a dipping fork to drop the truffles into the chocolate and toss to coat. Lift out and place on the baking parchment. Top with a dried strawberry immediately, before the chocolate sets.

★ **Makes 18 strawberry treats**

★ **Take 40 minutes to make; plus overnight chilling and 4 hours freezing.**

100g (3½oz) milk chocolate, broken into pieces
1 tbsp double cream
25g (1oz) unsalted butter, chopped
2 tbsp strawberry liqueur
White chocolate, for tempering
18 dried strawberries

Cream Tea Etiquette
Cornish Cream Tea – the strawberry jam goes on the scone before the cream. Devonshire Tea – the strawberry jam goes on top of the cream.

TEQUILA CHILLIES

★ **Makes 10 madly fabulous chillies**

★ **Take 40 minutes to make; plus 48 hours soaking and overnight chilling.**

8 mild or spicy green
    chillies
3 tbsp Silver Tequila
1 tbsp double cream
50g (2oz) white chocolate,
    chopped
Zest of ½ lime and a
    squeeze of lime juice
25g (1oz) unsalted butter,
    chopped
White chocolate, for
    tempering
About 1 tsp flaked sea salt

Sing-a-long
Whoa, the hokey cokey!
Whoa, the hokey cokey!
Knees bent, arms stretched.
Rah! Rah! Rah!

You put your chillies in,
Pour tequila out,
In out, in out,
Shake sea salt about.
You add the lime ganache and you turn around
That's what it's all about . . .

★ Don a pair of rubber gloves (otherwise your fingers will sting for days from doing this; anyway you know you love wearing rubber gloves) and cut a slit lengthways down the middle of each chilli and carefully take out the seeds. Put them in a sealable container and add 2 tablespoons of the Silver Tequila. Leave to soak for 48 hours – the soaking takes the sting out of the chillies.

★ Heat 5cm (2in) water in a pan. Pop a heatproof bowl on top of the pan, making sure the bottom of the bowl is not touching the water. Place the cream and chocolate in the bowl. Place over a gentle heat to allow the chocolate to melt.

★ Take the bowl off the heat and add the remaining tequila, the lime zest and juice and butter. Whisk everything until it becomes a smooth ganache, pour into a sealable container, then chill overnight to set.

★ When you are ready to fill the chillies, take a teaspoon and scoop up about half a teaspoon of ganache and stuff it into the chillies. Chill.

★ Temper the white chocolate (see page 13). Dip each chilli in the chocolate to cover, then sprinkle each with a little sea salt. Set them aside on a baking sheet covered with baking parchment to set.

HOT CHOCOLATE GROG

★ **Makes 2 x 125ml
(4½fl oz) pots/cups**

★ **Take 15 minutes to put
a smile on your face.**

100g (3½oz) dark
   chocolate
2 tsp rice flour
100ml (3½fl oz)
   full-fat milk
2 tsp rum
2 tbsp double cream
Demerara sugar,
   to sprinkle
2 good pinches of freshly
   grated nutmeg
2 cinnamon sticks

It is snowing. Winter has reached the ice-edged, fish-freezing pond, the headlong moon beams over the patchwork garden – white as snow, feather white. Tomorrow the children will plunge their mittens into the sticky-backed snow, laughing in the crisp, bell-pealing, carol-singing air. Small cats will walk the back garden fjord, print-making with their gentle feet. Men huddle at the wind-whipped corner, with their hands cupped around velvet-thick rum-laced chocolate, collars upturned to the cold. And look, there is Mrs Prothero cuckooing towards her ice-stiff, cold snapped, frozen crispy pancake washing, wreaths of breath misting around her curlers, calling for her cats.

★ Put the chocolate directly into a pan with 100ml (3½fl oz) cold water. Heat gently to melt the chocolate.
★ Add the rice flour and use a wooden spoon to mix all the ingredients together. Bring up to the boil, stirring all the time, until as thick as Dull Brian.
★ Slowly add the milk, just like you would when making a white or cheese sauce, and with the mixture still bubbling, whisk like the devil herself until smooth and thickened.
★ Open the rum bottle and take a swig for fortification. Stir 2 teaspoons of rum into the chocolate mixture, then whip it off the heat and divide it between two small cups.
★ Whisk the cream with a pinch of sugar in a bowl with a balloon whisk until just stiff. Divide among the pots. Sprinkle with Demerara and nutmeg, and serve each with a cinnamon stick. Lovely.

CHERRY CHEESECAKE CUPS

It is end of term at Rosey O'Conner's Hip and Thigh exercise class and leader Jenny has requested we all bring in a treat. Margaret brings a Tums and Bums Quiche Lorraine and Fat Sally brings a meat feast pizza with extra cheese. I decide to take my smashing Cherry Cheesecake Cups; a fluted milk chocolate cup filled with a cherry and cream cheesecake filling, because I am determined to keep off those extra pounds.

★ Put the cherries in a small bowl and add the kirsch. Cover and set aside for at least 8 hours. Do 100 sit-ups.

★ When the cherries have soaked, prepare the cups. Temper the chocolate (see page 13) and use a clean, grease-free brush or teaspoon to coat and line each of the fluted cups in the mould with the white chocolate. Do this quickly, partly to burn calories and partly because the chocolate will cool and become too thick to work with. Use a sharp knife to tidy up any bits around the chocolate shells. Chill for 20 minutes. Scrape any chocolate that you haven't used into a bowl and save to use again. Do 25 lunges.

★ Mix together the crushed biscuit and melted butter in a bowl. When the chocolate cases have set, gently upturn onto a board and set the right way up. Divide the biscuit mixture among the cups and press down with the back of a teaspoon very gently.

★ Beat together the cream cheese and icing sugar then fold in the cherries and any juicy bits still in the bowl with them. Spoon this over the digestive base.

★ Cut the whole glacé cherries in half then put a half on top of each chocolate. Run 3 miles.

★ **Makes 11 low-calorie cups**

★ **Take 30 minutes to make; plus chilling.**

25g (1oz) dried cherries, chopped
1 tbsp kirsch (cherry-flavoured brandy liqueur)
Milk chocolate, for tempering
1 digestive biscuit, crushed
10g (½oz) melted butter
3 level tbsp full-fat cream cheese
1 tsp icing sugar
5½ glacé cherries

11-hole fluted cup chocolate mould (please see the end of this book for stockists)

LIMONCELLO CREAMS

Limoncello is an Italian lemon liqueur made from the Sorrento lemon, which is grown in Southern Italy. These white-chocolate creams are filled with a divine zesty limoncello ganache. They are as pure as Katherine Hepburn in *Summer Madness* as she leans out from the Venice train, gardenia in hand, waving a tearful goodbye to Rossano Brazzi. Honestly, I could slap her silly face.

★ Heat 5cm (2in) water in a pan. Put a heatproof bowl on top of the pan, making sure the bottom of the bowl is not touching the water. Place the chocolate in the bowl with the cream and heat gently to allow the chocolate to melt.

★ Take the bowl off the heat and toss in the lemon zest, limoncello, salt and butter and whisk airy fairily until the mixture resembles homemade lemon curd. Try really hard not to make a round of toast. Spoon into a sealable container, put the lid on and chill overnight.

★ Scoop up small teaspoons of the mixture and roll into balls. Put on a board lined with baking parchment and freeze overnight.

★ Temper the white chocolate (see page 13). Use a round-headed dipping fork, or two common forks, to dip each truffle into the chocolate. Toss about blithely to coat, then lift out and place back on the parchment, roughening the chocolate with a fork. Repeat, then chill the chocolates to allow them to set.

★ **Makes 18 divine truffles**

★ **Take around 40 minutes to make; plus 2 nights chilling and freezing.**

100g (3½ oz) white chocolate
2 tbsp double cream
Zest of ½ lemon
1–2 tbsp limoncello liqueur
A pinch of salt
50g (2oz) unsalted butter, chopped
White chocolate, for tempering

Tip
Chocolate is usually at its best at room temperature; however, I recommend you eat these almost icy cold – like Rossano Brazzi's heart.

SHERRY TRIFLE CUPS

★ **Makes 11 Betty Bright cups**

★ **Take 45 minutes.**

White chocolate,
   for tempering
2 cubes raspberry jelly
50ml (2fl oz) double cream
A pinch of icing sugar
2 tsp Madeira
Hundreds and thousands,
   to decorate

11-hole fluted cup
   chocolate mould (please
   see the end of this book
   for stockists)

WHERE IS BETTY NOW?
Betty allegedly married Harold Bowden, whose father owned a bicycle company on Raleigh Street. Harry's Chopper is still legendary.

My grandfather's diary tells the story of Betty Bright, his first love, who caught his eye when demonstrating her extraordinary unicycle tricks outside the chip shop. Slipped into the back of her diary was Betty's recipe for sherry trifle. I have reworked her original recipe into the most splendidly delicate chocolate 'cup' – with real jelly and Madeira cream.

★ Temper the white chocolate (see page 13) and use a clean, grease-free brush or teaspoon to coat and thickly line each of the fluted cups in the mould with the white chocolate. Go to it as quick as a stick otherwise the chocolate will cool and become too thick to work with. Use a sharp knife to tidy up any raggedy bits around the chocolate shells. Chill for 20 minutes. Scrape any white chocolate that you haven't used into a bowl and save to use again.
★ Chop up the jelly and put in a bowl with 2 tablespoons boiling water. Whisk furiously, to melt the jelly, then set aside until cold but not quite set, just a bit wibbly-wobbly.
★ Take the white chocolate cups from the mould by gently upturning onto a board. Then set them the right way up. Spoon the cooled jelly equally among the white chocolate cups. Chill to set.
★ Beat the cream in a bowl until thick, then fold in the icing sugar and Madeira. Spoon the mixture over the jelly-filled cups then sprinkle with hundreds and thousands. Down in one and don't spare the horses.

GIN AND TONIC TRUFFLES

★ **Makes 20 banging truffles**

★ **Take around 30 minutes to make; plus overnight chilling.**

100g (3½oz) dark chocolate, broken into pieces
2 tbsp double cream
2 tbsp gin
Zest and juice of ½ lime
50g (2oz) unsalted butter, chopped
Cocoa powder, to dust

Here I have craftily concealed a tipple of gin inside a luscious dark chocolate truffle with a wicked twist of fresh lime. It carries a punch akin to that of Bert Bantam the 8-stone featherweight boxer from Eccles, who unexpectedly knocked out the Giant of Redcar, Mr Arthur Whitlow, at the 1953 Pigeon and Ferret Fanciers Fair with just a single blow to the left buttock.

★ Heat 5cm (2in) water in a pan. Put a heatproof bowl on top of the pan, making sure the bottom of the bowl is not touching the water. Whap the chocolate in the bowl with the cream and heat gently to allow the chocolate to melt.

★ Tipple in the gin, lime zest and juice and the butter. Whisk the ingredients together until smooth and slightly thickened. Spoon into a sealable container, snap on the lid and chill overnight.

★ Take teaspoons of the mixture and roll into balls. Put on a board lined with baking parchment and chill for an hour or so. *Build a Boat in your Front Room* is on the telly followed by *Divorce on the High Seas*.

★ Sieve the cocoa into a bowl and roll the truffles in it to cover.

★ Eat them and text ex-boyfriends.

HOUSEHOLD USES FOR GIN
Gin is excellent for making things vanish. Simply drink half a bottle and watch irritating husbands and children with maths homework disappear.

HOPE AND GREENWOOD

Ladies' Afternoon Tea

CHAPTER FIVE

SPLENDID CONFECTIONERY

MY MUM'S FAIRY PRINCESS CAKES

★ **Makes 24 fluffy cakes**

★ **Take 40 minutes to make.**

110g (4oz) softened
  unsalted butter
110g (4oz) golden caster
  sugar
2 medium eggs
75g (3oz) self-raising flour
2 tbsp cocoa powder
A good splash of semi-
  skimmed milk

For the decoration
25g (1oz) softened
  unsalted butter
75g (3oz) icing sugar,
  plus extra to dust
1 tbsp cocoa powder
1–2 tbsp semi-skimmed
  milk
Gold lustre, to dust
  (please see the end of
  this book for stockists)

24-hole mini-muffin tin

On Sunday afternoons Mum was in the kitchen making cakes from the Bero Cook Book and Dad was beating the mixture with a wooden spoon and a lot of elbow grease. Here are my Mum's Fairy Princess Cakes – chocolatey, fluffy, and right proper. Mum, I'm very sorry, I have added twinkles. Consider this payback for making me wear that hideous cherry hat on Tunstall Bank when I was 14.

★ Preheat the oven to 180°C/350°F/Gas 4. Line a mini-muffin tin with paper cases. Put the butter and sugar in a large bowl and cream together using an electric hand whisk or a dad-sized wooden spoon. Whisk in the eggs, then fold in the flour and cocoa. Splash in a decent sploosh of milk, so that the mix drops off the spoon with ease.
★ Plop a bit of the mix into each paper case and bake for 15 minutes. Cool on a wire rack.
★ Now for the icing. Beat the butter in a bowl and gradually add the icing sugar, then fold in the cocoa and milk.
★ Using a small sharp knife, cut the top off each cake then cut them in half – these will be the fairy wings. Use a knife to spread a little of the icing on top then pop the two cake halves on top of each cake to make wings. Dust with icing sugar and glorify with a little gold lustre.

CHOCOLATE AND PISTACHIO PALMIERS

The word 'palmier' literally means 'palm tree', as indeed these chocolate-filled, sugar caramelised, crispy, puff pastry treats look rather like palm fronds. Tragically, they are also known as 'elephant's ears' and 'pig's ears'. I almost cried a little.

★ Line two 39 x 35cm (15¼ x 13¾in) baking sheets with greaseproof paper.

★ Dust a clean work surface with flour. Roll the oblong of puff pastry to make a rectangle measuring about 28 x 18cm (11 x 7in). Roll the pastry one way only, otherwise the puff pastry won't rise evenly; now that is what I call a handy hint.

★ Spread the pastry with the Nutella then scatter over the pistachios. Press them into the Nutella. Roll the longest sides in towards each other until they meet in the middle, pressing the pastry down firmly as you go. Press the two joins together, then turn over and pop on one of the lined baking sheets. Chill for 20–30 minutes. Preheat the oven to 220°C/425°F/Gas 7.

★ Take the pastry roll out of the fridge and put it on a board. Slice it into 5mm–1cm (¼–½in) pieces from one end, working down to the other. Lay the pastry flat-side down on the prepared greaseproof, then lightly roll each one with the rolling pin to flatten. Sprinkle with sugar, then bake in the oven for 10–15 minutes until golden and crisp.

★ **Makes 22 frondy biscuits**

★ **Take 30 minutes to make; plus chilling.**

A little flour for rolling out
½ x 500g pack puff pastry
4–5 level tbsp Nutella
25g (1oz) pistachios, finely chopped
Golden granulated sugar, to sprinkle

ROSE QUEEN PROFITEROLES

★ **Makes 12 fragrant profiteroles**

★ **Take 45 minutes to make, plus 18 hours chained to the railings.**

40g (1 ½oz) butter, chilled and cubed
60g (2 ½oz) plain flour, sifted
1 medium egg

For the filling and topping
75g (3oz) white chocolate
150ml pot double cream
½ tbsp rosewater
1 tbsp icing sugar
Crystallised rose petals

My granny was lucky enough to be chosen as a Rose Queen during Queen Alexandra's London tour in 1917. In her excitement to hand over her basket of roses she came close to being trampled, suffragette style, by the Queen's horses.

Later, with two broken arms, she went home and ironed my Grandad's pants and deloused his toupee.

★ Preheat the oven to 200°C/400°F/Gas 6. Line a baking sheet with baking parchment. Flutter around the kitchen practising your royal wave.

★ Put the butter in a pan with 110ml (4fl oz) cold water. Melt over a low heat then bring to a really fast boil. As soon as this happens, remove from the heat. Add all the flour and beat vigorously. Leave to cool.

★ Beat the egg in a bowl and add it, a little at a time, to the cooled mixture. Keep adding enough to make the mixture as smooth and glossy as a queen's ballgown.

★ Take a wet teaspoon and spoon half teaspoonfuls of the mixture onto the baking parchment (this helps the mixture slip off easily) to make 12 balls.

★ Bake in the oven for 25 minutes until golden. Remove from the oven, use a skewer or sharp knife to stick a hole in the side of each one. Return to the oven for a few minutes. Thus the profiteroles will be cooked properly – soggy profiteroles are awfully plebeian. Cool on a wire rack.

P.T.O.

★ Heat 5cm (2in) water in a pan. Pop a heatproof bowl on top of the pan, making sure the bottom of the bowl is not touching the water. Plonk the chocolate in the bowl and allow it to melt – don't stir it, please don't, darling.

★ Beat the cream with the rosewater and icing sugar in a bowl until thick and sumptuous.

★ Split the profiteroles and fill with the rosewater cream – you can do this with a piping bag, if you like, a spoon or your thumb, if you are ill equipped. Spoon the melted chocolate on top. Sprinkle with crystallised rose petals and leave to set. Enjoy immediately if instant gratification is your thang. They will be tickety-boo, unfilled, for two or three days if stored in an airtight container.

PROFITEROLE ETIQUETTE
Do not lick the cream out of the middle – you really are such a Bargain Bucket peasant.

ROYAL MILE COBBLES

I shall tell you of my chum, Mr William Wallace, who regularly receives a wee parcel of my dangerous, dark chocolate, nutty, fruity, mallow-studded Royal Mile Cobbles. On St Andrew's Day he dresses up as Mel Gibson and, cobble in hand, performs a whirling jig. Grainy webcam images reveal the secrets of his under kilt. Hold, ladies, h-o-l-d.

★ Grease and line a 20cm (8in) square tin with baking parchment.
★ Heat 5cm (2in) water in a pan. Pop a heatproof bowl on top of the pan, making sure the bottom of the bowl is not touching the water. Place the chocolate in the bowl with the butter and allow to melt.
★ Add the marshmallows, mixed nuts and dates to the chocolate and stir everything gently together like your life depended on it.
★ Tip into the tin, leveling the chocolatey cement down as you go, like a cable tosser, then fling a few extra mini marshmallows over the top with Highland abandon. Chill for at least 30 minutes. Remove from the tin and peel away the paper. Crown with the gold leaf.
★ Cut into chunks, triangles, squares, thistles, haggis — whatever you fancy — and pile them up castle-like on a plate to serve.

★ **Makes around 20 man-sized chunks**

★ **Take 15 minutes to make; plus 30 minutes chilling.**

A little oil for greasing
300g (11oz) dark
    chocolate, chopped
75g (3oz) unsalted butter
110g (4oz) mini
    marshmallows or large
    ones, quartered, plus
    extra to decorate
200g (7oz) mixed nuts,
    such as brazils,
    hazelnuts and pecans,
    roughly chopped
110g (4oz) dates, chopped
Edible gold leaf (please
    see the end of this book
    for stockists)

Handy Hint
A Scotsman's thighs are traditionally wider than a girder. Squeeeeeeeal.

EARL GREY TEA CUP MOUSSE

★ **Makes 4 velvety cups**

★ **Take 20 minutes to make; plus 2 hours chilling.**

4 Earl Grey tea bags, plus a few leaves from a bag to garnish
150g (5oz) milk chocolate, plus extra to make curls (you might need a spare bar for this – does a 'spare bar' actually exist?)
150ml (5fl oz) each single cream and double cream, plus around 100ml (3½fl oz) extra double cream, to decorate
1 large egg, separated
1 tbsp golden caster sugar

There is lot of drivel written about the origins of Earl Grey tea. To put the history books straight, Earl Grey was a New York Jazz musician and a member of the Harlem Syncopators. He loved a cup of builders' and was famous for his songs, 'Chattanooga Brew Brew', 'I Get a Kick Out of Brew' and, posthumously, 'It's my Tea Party and I'll Cry if I Want to.'

★ Pour 50ml (2fl oz) boiling water into a jug and add the tea bags. Leave to steep for 5 minutes. Toss the bags binwards.
★ Heat 5cm (2in) water in a pan. Plonk a heatproof bowl on top of the pan, making sure the bottom of the bowl is not touching the water. Place the chocolate in the bowl and allow to melt – don't stir it otherwise it may turn into a thick mess. Remove the bowl from the pan and cool a tad.
★ Stir in the single cream, the tea and the egg yolk. Whisk the egg white in a clean, grease-free bowl until stiff peaks appear. Beat the double cream in a separate bowl until thick (there's no need to wash the whisks if you do it this way round – you domestic slut, you).
★ Fold the double cream into the other ingredients and then, finally, fold in the beaten egg white. Divide equally among four teacups, cover, then chill for at least 2 hours. Brasso your saxophone whilst waiting.
★ When ready to serve, whip the remaining 100ml (3½fl oz) double cream in a bowl until thick then fold in the sugar. Spoon into each teacup and sprinkle a few Earl Grey tea leaves on top. Use a peeler to scrape along the remaining milk chocolate to make curls and sprinkle them over the cream. Serve immediately.

PINK FANCIES

I have tried to embrace the understated shade of olive and have opened myself up to the temptations of taupe, but to no avail – they are just too dull. I like pink, pretty pink. Especially when it is a Pink Fancy made of feather-light sponge, filled with rich buttercream and wrapped in a cloak of pink icing.

★ Preheat the oven to 170°C/325°F/Gas 3. Grease and line a 20cm (8in) square cake tin with greaseproof paper.
★ Cream the butter and sugar together in a bowl. Beat in the eggs, adding a little of the plain flour if the mixture looks like it will curdle.
★ Fold in the flours, milk and grated chocolate. Spoon into the tin and bake for 50 minutes until a skewer inserted into the centre comes out clean. Remove the cake from the tin and cool on a wire rack.
★ To make the buttercream, beat the butter and icing sugar in a bowl until soft. Stir in the milk so the mixture is a bit sloppy.
★ Cut the cake into 25 squares. Cut each square in half horizontally, like a sarni, then spread a thin layer of buttercream on each base and sandwich together with the top. Allow the buttercream to set.
★ Make up the fondant according to the packet instructions. Rest a cake rack on a board or baking sheet. Lift the cakes up and spoon the icing around the sides of the cakes first. Place the cakes on the rack, then spoon over some icing to cover the top. This is quite a messy job.
★ When all the squares are covered, decorate each with a sugar flower and leave to set. Serve in little paper cases.

★ **Makes 25 fancy pink cakes**

★ **Take 1 hour 45 minutes to make.**

150g (5oz) softened unsalted butter
150g (5oz) caster sugar
2 large eggs, beaten
50g (2oz) plain flour, sifted
125g (4½oz) self-raising flour, sifted
A good splash of semi-skimmed milk
50g (2oz) grated white chocolate

For the icing
25g (1oz) softened butter
75g (3oz) icing sugar
½–1 tbsp semi-skimmed milk
1 box set of Real Fruit Fondant Icing (please see the end of this book for stockists)
Rice paper sugar flowers (please see the end of this book for stockists)

MR ROMARY'S VICTORY BISCUITS

★ **Makes 8 crown-shaped biscuits**

★ **Take 1 hour to make; including chilling time.**

100g (3½oz) softened butter, plus extra for greasing
25g (1oz) rolled oats
40g (1½oz) caster sugar
50g (2oz) wholemeal flour, sifted
75g (3oz) plain flour, sifted, plus extra for rolling out
75g (3oz) milk chocolate
Coloured sprinkles

A crown cutter (please see the end of this book for stockists)

MR ROMARY LIVES ON
Sadly, Mr Romary's bakery closed in 1963. The last official batch of biscuits was baked for Charles and Diana's wedding in 1981.

Mr Romary opened his bakery in Tunbridge Wells, England, in 1862, where he made the finest biscuits in the land. Queen Victoria loved them so much she popped in in person in 1876, heralding the birth of Mr Romary's famous 'Victory' biscuit. Apparently she was quite amused.

★ Grease and line two baking sheets with greaseproof paper.
★ Whiz the rolled oats in a posh mini blender briefly or chop with a peasant's knife.
★ Beat the butter and sugar together in a bowl until soft. Add the chopped oats and flours and stir together until the mixture looks crumbly. Roll up your sleeves and knead the crumbs until they become a lump of dough. Wrap in greaseproof and chill for 15 minutes.
★ Preheat the oven to 170°C/325°F/Gas 3. Roll out on a lightly floured surface and stamp out crowns, rerolling the dough where necessary. Put the biscuits on the prepared baking sheets and bake for 15–20 minutes until golden round the edges. Cool on a wire rack.
★ Heat 5cm (2in) water in a pan. Put a heatproof bowl on top of the pan, making sure the bottom of the bowl is not touching the water. Place the chocolate in the bowl and heat gently to melt.
★ Use a dessertspoon to drizzle the chocolate randomly over the biscuits then cover with sprinkles.
★ Store in an airtight container and eat within three days. Hip, hip!

MISS HOPE'S CHOCOLATE BOX LADIES' AFTERNOON TEA

ROSE GARDEN CAKE

When we were children we were so ashamed of our front garden that my sister and I cut the grass with nail scissors. Nowadays, my newly green-fingered mother has pictures of Alan Titchmarsh on her fridge, a pensioner's pass to Wisley and a hemp bag from Kew. She also makes the most beautiful, rich chocolate cake topped with frosting and laden with her garden roses.

★ Preheat the oven to 180°C/350°F/Gas 4. Grease and line the ceramic pots or traditional 20cm (8in) round cake tin if you prefer.
★ Put the butter, dark chocolate and 100ml (3½fl oz) water straight into a pan and heat to melt the butter and chocolate. Stir together and set aside to cool.
★ Sift the flour and cocoa into a bowl. Stir in the sugars. In a separate large bowl, beat the eggs.
★ Pour the chocolate mixture into the bowl with the eggs and 75ml (3fl oz) yogurt. Stir everything together – you may need to add the extra 25ml (1fl oz) yogurt at this stage if the mixture is very stiff. Spoon into the prepared pots or tin. Bake the pots for 45 minutes– 1 hour or the tin for 50 minutes–1 hour. Remove and cool completely on a wire rack.
★ To make the buttercream, beat the butter and icing sugar in a bowl until soft and creamy. Stir in the milk and vanilla extract just to slacken the mixture. Spread the mixture over the cakes.
★ Cover each cake with the roses.

★ **Makes 4 cakes; each serves 2**

★ **Take around 1 hour 30 minutes to make.**

110g (4oz) unsalted butter, plus extra to grease
75g bar dark chocolate, chopped
225g (8oz) self-raising flour
25g (1oz) cocoa powder, sifted
150g (5oz) each golden caster sugar and light brown soft sugar
2 medium eggs
75–100ml (3–4fl oz) natural yogurt

For the decoration
200g (7oz) softened unsalted butter
600g (1lb 5oz) icing sugar
1–2 tbsp semi-skimmed milk
1 tsp vanilla extract
4 x 11cm ceramic flower pots or a 20cm (8in) round tin
Fresh unsprayed roses

GOOD LUCK WEDDING MERINGUES

★ **Makes 8 girlie meringues, serves 4**

★ **Take 1 hour 20 minutes to make.**

1 medium egg white
50g (2oz) caster sugar
2 tsp cocoa powder, sieved
100ml (3½fl oz) double
 cream
1 tsp icing sugar
8 chocolate silver coins,
 to decorate

A Little Poem:

Something old,
something new,
Something borrowed,
something blue,
And a sixpence for
luck in her shoe.

My mum made these little chocolate meringues for special occasions, adding a real silver sixpence for good luck. As I am not suggesting you inflict the Heimlich Manoeuvre on Auntie Doris, please use a foiled chocolate sixpence instead.

★ Preheat the oven to 120°C/250°F/Gas ½. Line a 39 × 35cm (15¼ × 13¾in) baking sheet with baking parchment.
★ Pop the egg white in a spotlessly clean, grease-free bowl (washing up helps). Whisk with an electric hand whisk until stiff peaks form, or give it a good thrashing with a balloon whisk. It's ready when you can turn the bowl upside down over your head and it doesn't move.
★ Add half the caster sugar and continue to whisk in until smooth and glossy. This is exceptionally good for your hips. Then add the remaining sugar, teaspoon by teaspoon, until it's all incorporated into the egg white. Sprinkle over the cocoa and fold it in to ripple through the meringue in a streaky manner.
★ Use a large tablespoon to spoon eight even-sized blobettes onto the baking parchment then bake them in the oven for 45 minutes– 1 hour until the meringues come away from the sheet. Cool.
★ When ready to serve, whip the cream in a bowl until thick. Fold in the icing sugar. Use the cream to sandwich together the meringues and pop a silver coin in the cream. Serve immediately.

JEWELLED FLORENTINES

★ **Makes around
24 biscuits**

★ **Take 40 minutes
to make.**

40g (1½oz) mixed dried
   fruit, such as soured
   cherries, pineapple,
   blueberries and
   crystallised angelica
40g (1½oz) mixed nuts,
   such as hazelnuts and
   almonds, chopped
2 tsp rice flour
50g (2oz) plain flour
1 tbsp golden syrup
50g (2oz) golden caster
   sugar
50g (2oz) unsalted butter
110g (4oz) white chocolate

Giacomo Moretti insisted that his favourite baker deliver
these cherry, pineapple, blueberry and angelica Florentines to
his dressing room at the opera house in Florence. He famously
coined the phrase: 'Leave the gun, take the Florentines'.

★ Preheat the oven to 180°C/350°F/Gas 4. Line a couple of
39 x 35cm (15¼ x 13¾in) baking sheets with baking parchment.
★ Introduce the fruit and angelica to your favourite mixing bowl
and toss in the nuts. Add the flours and jiggle everything together.
I know you know how.
★ Put the golden syrup, sugar and butter in a pan and heat gently
to dissolve the sugar and melt the butter. Simmer for 1 minute.
★ Pour this toffee mixture into the bowl and stir together. Spoon
half teaspoons of the mixture onto the parchment and bake for
around 12 minutes until golden. Cool on the baking sheet until firm
enough to lift, then use a palette knife to transfer them to a wire rack.
★ Heat 5cm (2in) water in a pan. Pop a heatproof bowl on top of the
pan, making sure the bottom of the bowl is not touching the water.
Place the chocolate in the bowl and melt it gently – don't stir it
otherwise it may turn into a thick mess.
★ Spoon a little chocolate onto the base of each Florentine and
smooth to cover. Leave until almost set, then use a fork to make
a wavy pattern down the middle of the white chocolate. Leave
to set completely.

Trivia

Moretti's opera career was
tragically cut short after being hit
by a tram while crossing the road
to the bakers. Bada bing.

MISS HOPE'S CHOCOLATE BOX LADIES' AFTERNOON TEA

STOCKISTS

I realise that some of the ingredients and equipment in this book may be a bit tricky to track down, so here is a list of lovely stockists – you can order online, by phone or take a trip to town.

HOPE AND GREENWOOD
www.hopeandgreenwood.co.uk
Tel: 020 8613 1777
The finest dark, milk and white chocolate bars, chocolate-covered coffee beans, fluffy marshmallows, chocolate silver sixpences, fabulous fudge, nougat and just about anything your heart could desire.

JANE ASHER
www.jane-asher.co.uk
Callebaut milk, dark and white couverture.

CONFISERIE FLORIAN
www.confiserieflorian.co.uk
Rose syrup.

THE DRINK SHOP
www.thedrinkshop.com
Tel: 01843 570571
Frangelica, Silver Tequila, Chambord, crème de cassis, green ginger wine, Bramley and Gage strawberry liqueur, limoncello, kirsch – hangover.

FORTNUM AND MASON
www.fortnumandmason.com
Tel: 020 7734 8040
Crystallised rose petals and cystallised angelica, tea, and a day out really.

JULIAN GRAVES
www.juliangraves.com
Tel: 0845 602 4816
Fruits and nuts:
Strawberries, pine nuts, Medjool dates, Agen prunes, dried mango, pistachios, candied orange peel, hazelnuts, walnuts, brazils, hazelnuts, pecans and sour cherries.

HEALTHY SUPPLIES
www.healthysupplies.co.uk
Dried raspberry bits and dried strawberries.

LAKELAND
www.lakeland.co.uk
Tel: 015394 88100
Baking tins and sugar thermometers, plus a whole host of things you didn't know you needed.

SQUIRES
www.squires-shop.com
Tel: 0845 61 71 810
For food stuffs:
Real fruit fondant icing, gold lustre, edible gold leaf, chocolate sprinkles, such as vermicelli or flakes, and silver balls.

Also for equipment:
Wooden lolly sticks, muffin cases and petit four cases, dipping forks for posh people, sugar thermometers. Chocolate moulds including: 11-hole fluted cups, 9-hole butterflies, bite-sized hearts, lips, seashell assortments, and also crown biscuit cutters.

SUPERMARKETS
Sainsburys/Tesco
Madeira cake, chocolate sprinkles – vermicelli and flakes, sponge fingers, glucose syrup, rice paper, Camp Coffee Essence, elderflower cordial, dark muscovado sugar, Maldon Sea Salt, stem ginger in syrup, rice paper, Billington's dark glacé cherries, trolley rage.

Waitrose/Ocado
www.ocado.com
Tel: 0845 399 1122
Agen prunes, mini marshmallows, rosewater, Amaretti biscuits, Valrhona couverture.

INDEX

THANK YOUS

With special thanks to my mother for indulging my sister and me with her crusts-off, silver-tea-pot, Ladies' Afternoon Tea.

Thanks to Emma for all her help and advice. Thanks to Elinor my tenacious agent.

Big it up for my chum Kano — the voice of Squirrel Greenwood (I am so down, yo' feel me?).

And to Mr Greenwood who I can safely say, once again, did absolutely nothing at all.

And a big thank you to Teddy, my editor, for allowing me every crudity — except the one about penuche being the Spanish for lady love ears.